The 'I' in Me
Who Am I Anyway?

Authored by Kamarun Kalam

(BACP Accredited & Social Work England Reg)

BA Hons Social Work & DipSW/ Dip Counselling

Founder of Talkwellcounselling.co.uk

Dedicated To

This book is dedicated to my beautiful family: my three children, Lamees, Maryam and Adam, who have been a constant source of learning, fascination and love and my husband Kalam, who has offered his unwavering support throughout this whole process and kept me grounded and motivated.

My pet parrot Coco also deserves some credit; he has lightened up my life with his chirpy bird songs, funny little sentences and dances. I must also mention all of my clients past and present who continue to educate me in the art of therapy, as I learn and grow with each one.

It has taken a team of people to produce this book and each of the above-named people deserve recognition for supporting me through this process.

Acknowledgements

I would like to offer my sincerest gratitude and thanks to my dear childhood friend Emma Jackson for supporting me in the early stages of preparing this book. Emma provided me with the encouragement, practical advice and guidance I needed, and I am eternally grateful for it. A special thanks to my daughter Maryam who used her talent in art to support me with the illustrations in this book.

I offer thanks to God who has helped me throughout my journey in life so far.

Table of Contents

Introduction

"Who died and made someone else the boss of you?"

Trying to be someone you are not just to keep another person in your life really doesn't pay; you end up getting used or growing resentful, then eventually you lose yourself in the process. Takers take and givers give. Which one are you? Come to think of it, do you even know who you are? I mean, really know? If I was to ask you right now on the spot, "Who are you?" I bet you would reel off a load of labels; mother, father, worker, student, etc. That isn't who you are; it's one of many roles you play. I want you to dig deeper and reflect on who you really are. Read on to explore what factors went into making you who you are today.

The 'I' in 'Me'

(Knowing, Accepting & Loving your Authentic Self)

Hi there! My name is Kam, and as a counsellor and social worker I would like to share with you my passion and curiosity regarding the human condition. I have a keen interest in understanding all aspects of the self: physical, emotional, psychological and spiritual. I believe we are all connected as a human family and our similarities far outweigh our differences. After all, is it not love, belonging, acceptance and affection we all seek in life?

I find it fascinating to learn from others and see reflected back their personal journeys through therapy. What is evident is that our identities are essentially who we are, but what makes up our individuality? What ingredients, if you like, go into making each and every one of us so different?

Suffice to say, we are not just defined by our names, ages or roles we play in life; we are a sum of many parts, which makes each and every one of us distinctively unique. This book has been designed to make you think, reflect on, and appreciate the diversity of life within yourself and others—to really focus on the 'I' inside you that is often unheard, forgotten or ignored. We are made up of so many different selves over time and change through life experiences. I'm guessing the views or values you held as a teenager have changed as you entered into adulthood and will continue to change over the course of your life as you grow, mature, and develop.

Your personality evolves over time as does your lifestyle, and there are many aspects that have gone into making you who you are today. Your physical, emotional, psychological, intellectual, social, cultural, religious and sexual selves are the sum parts of the total of you.

This is not an exhaustive list; there are many other factors that make us unique—our age, gender, class and economic status, for example. Our personal experiences in life shape who we are, how we think and how we behave towards others. We all share a natural curiosity to learn more about ourselves and others in order to enrich and enhance our personal and professional relationships.

I would like to invite you to reflect on your own personal journeys in life. To celebrate the diversity of life and appreciation of the self and all it encompasses—the beauty of being you. You never know; you might just inspire yourself! Oh, and just a quick note to say that this book was written to be read easily, with the intention of getting you actively engaged and completing the exercises in the book to start addressing things right from the get-go. I also love using quotes, so look out for those pearls of wisdom scattered throughout the book .

"I am a different person to different people, but who am I to me?" (Kam)

Tip: invest in a journal in which you can document your personal journey of change. This book is packed with questions, exercises and activities. So, treat yourself to a fancy pen and notebook that you will enjoy using. The act of writing is quite therapeutic in itself.

Chapter 1

The Theory Bit...

There was once a man called George Herbert Mead—he was born in 1863 and was an American philosopher, Psychologist and Sociologist. Mead developed a theory around the concept of self, called "Social Behaviourism", which states that one's identity emerges out of external social interactions and internal feelings of oneself. The 'self' is not evident at birth but emerges over time through language, play, and games. The self consists of 'Me' and 'I'. The 'I' is the un-socialised baby who is full of wants, needs and desires. 'Me' is the more grown-up socialised self, who has experienced life in relation to others and learned to live in society.

The theory of the social self is based on the argument that the self is a social thing. There are three activities through which the self is developed:

1. Language

2. Play

3. Game

Language allows the person to understand the role of the other, helping them to respond to the other's gestures. Play allows the individual to "take on the role of others" (pretend or role playing) so that they can learn to express the expectations of significant others. Game allows the individual to comprehend the rules of the "game", or, social interactions.

Basically, the 'self' has two sides. The 'Me' represents the expectations and attitudes of others that are assumed by the individual; it's the external you that is presented to the world, influenced by others. The 'I' is the response to the 'Me', or the person's individuality; the internal voice, if you like. Confused yet? Let me explain...

The self has two parts: self-awareness and a self-image. To explore this further, we need to appreciate that this theory of the 'self' is completely social. We do not focus on any kind of biological development of the personality. The self is something that comes from social interaction.

This theory highlights the self as social and not as biological. There is another social concept that correlates called the 'looking-glass self' to refer to significant people in our lives. (I'll discuss this later.)

Our sense of self and our understanding of who we are, what we like, and what our personality is becomes constructed through being in the world, through interaction with ourselves and being influenced by others socially. Therefore, the self is developed as we age and grow; as we experience life in relationship with others. It's not something innately biological—it's learnt, taught, and experienced in real time. The 'I' is the "born" you. The 'Me' is the "socialized" you.

To illustrate this point, you are born male/female. You are then socialized into certain behaviours and take on the beliefs of those around you. These are primarily views and beliefs of your caregivers, parents, siblings, teachers, etc. So, you may become exposed to stereotypical views and learn how to 'behave' as a male or a female; for example, "boys don't cry" or "girls don't play in the dirt".

To illustrate this point further, imagine you were in a car accident—not a serious one, just a small bumper scratch, but it was caused by another driver. The 'I', which is what's happening inside, might react with a rapid heartbeat, sweating, a sense of fear and shock, etc. The 'Me', which is the external self, may react by pulling over and swearing, getting angry or upset, then exchanging insurance details etc. See the difference?

"Authenticity – is the courage to be yourself regardless of who is around." (Kam)

For the purposes of this book, I will use the example of a schoolteacher to illustrate how this theory works. Imagine a primary school teacher called Joan. She would identify 'Me' as the teacher self, and 'I' as the person behind this, the one that enjoys teaching and helping others and has her own hopes, desires and vulnerabilities that are not necessarily on display.

The 'I' is the authentic self, the one that wears no masks. This concept can be applied to you and everybody else. Basically, the self develops through interacting with others, through reflecting on those interactions and how others view you. This helps to generate an image of yourself. A self-concept, if you like. This process unfolds as follows:

We experience being in this world by living amongst others, by being influenced by others and learning how to behave from a young age by watching our parents and significant others. So, how might these social interactions give rise to the self? Living in the world amongst a community allows us to have interactions and express our developing personalities to see how the self that we put out there on display for others is being reacted to. Our social mask, you could say; the parts of ourselves we readily show others in social settings are usually our 'best behaviour' masks. People may wear different masks for different occasions.

Stop for a second and have a think… How many masks do you wear? Do you change your personality around different people or do you remain the same whoever you are around?

"What gives it its human character is that the individual through language addresses himself in the role of the others in the group and thus becomes aware of them in his own conduct." (George Herbert Mead)

Exercise:

I want you to consider now and make some notes in your journal:

- How are others reacting to you (the 'me')?
- Do people praise who you are or what you do?
- Or do others put you down and tell you that you are useless?
- What labels have others given you that you now believe to be true   about yourself?

Remember that earlier I mentioned the concept of the 'looking-glass self'. Well, in this, the 'self' is mirrored in the reactions of the other. It is evident in babies who mirror their parents' faces when happy, angry or sad. You watch a mother smiling at her young baby—that smile is reflected back at her from the child automatically.

Imagine this (go back in time mentally and visualise your school days): You are a young, impressionable child sitting with a group of classmates discussing a project. To lighten the mood you make a jokey statement that makes everyone laugh, but then someone calls you an idiot and the group start laughing at you instead. This could impact your self-esteem negatively; you might start seeing yourself as an 'idiot' by internalising that belief but it's not yours—it came from an outside source, yet you may begin to believe it and act on it.

You adopt the 'looking glass' (others' beliefs about you), the mirror image of yourself that is being put back to you by others. You may believe what others say about you until it becomes a self-fulfilling prophecy, particularly if these patterns have a repeating effect and, on several occasions, you are called similar negative names. This will just reinforce that negative belief about yourself.

You may develop a self-image or self-concept that is tainted by that belief that was never yours to begin with but became ingrained by others into you. If these patterns get repeated again and again through your lifetime, you develop an image of yourself that is given to you not from your own frame of reference but from others. This is what we refer to as the 'looking-glass self'. It is other people's version of who you are that you adopt and is not your own.

The 'looking-glass self' was given to us by Charles Horton Cooley, an American Sociologist and Psychologist born in 1864. He developed the concept in 1902 and believed that everybody is susceptible to this behaviour, as we can so easily influence others within a social context. Through the lens of this theory, we can see how many people are living their lives believing themselves to be the sum total of what others have told them they are, without truly reflecting on it or challenging it. Not knowing their true selves but instead believing in a version of themselves portrayed as if mirrored back on them by others.

At this point, I need you to question. Who is really in charge of you? Have you allowed others to have power over you and criticise who you are? If so, then this book is perfect for you to rediscover who you truly are for yourself, by yourself, and without those critical voices. As children, we struggle to comprehend our individuality and strive to get recognition from friends, to fit in, to belong, to be accepted and liked so much so that we often lose our own identities in the process. Therefore, I ask you with the utmost sincerity… Who are you?

Wearing negative labels and harbouring negative or positive views about ourselves depends largely on the messages we received from others as we grew up. We then become that 'naughty boy' at school or the 'class clown' or the 'drama queen'; these labels often shape our personalities and we grow with them into adulthood. Significant adults such as parents, teachers, aunts, uncles and grandparents often have the most powerful influences on us as children, and often what they say is gospel to us; we swallow it whole without question, believing that we really are all those things they said about us.

Think back to your childhood. Maybe you heard messages like, '*You are fat, stupid, ugly, useless, thick, won't ever amount to anything*'. Such powerful negative messages on young minds can play havoc with a child's personal development. In contrast, with caregivers who nurture and stimulate children positively with remarks like, '*Well done, you are amazing, we are so proud of you, we love you'*—such children develop a healthier self-concept. Their belief system is boosted with confidence whereas their negative counterparts are degraded and shamed.

It is so important to be mindful of what we say to our children and each other as parents because words really do count; they can have lifelong consequences for those who hear us and believe what we say. Always try to nurture a sense of confidence, love and trust in children, and they in turn will believe in themselves and thrive.

As children we all crave our parents' attention, love, acceptance and validation. When this isn't forthcoming, we act out in different ways. Some withdraw and lose confidence and self-esteem. Others rebel and become disruptive as a defence mechanism, acting like nothing matters. Some turn to friends and create their own bubble of safety and acceptance through peers. It is only when we reflect back on our own childhoods that we see how we ended up becoming who we are today.

I remember completing my GCSE's and getting an A* in English and running home to tell my dad, as he was really big on education. Guess what his response was...? "You could have done better." Nothing seemed good enough; his standards were so high and I never quite got the validation I needed. I knew he loved me but I also kept trying to be better, so that one day he would be proud of me. This fed into my need to strive for perfection to keep working hard and not give up despite myself. (It goes a long way to explaining how I developed into a workaholic for years.)

Nothing was enough, and the bar was so high that I had inadvertently set myself up to fail. It was only through my training to become a Psychotherapist that I found balance and decided enough was enough. Years of working on the front line as a child protection social worker— trying to be good enough by overworking and overachieving, all to the detriment of my own family's well-being and health—made me stop in my tracks and reassess where I was going in life. I decided I could still help others but in a calmer setting and with more intensive support as a Counsellor. So, I began my labour of love of four years training and a further three years practice to become accredited by the BACP (British Association for Counsellors and Psychotherapists).

I never quite got that "I'm proud of you" statement from my dad; it would have been nice to hear it once in a while. His lack of capacity to express this says more about him and his upbringing than about me or my worthiness to receive validation. But as a child, I couldn't comprehend such adult themes. I only discovered this fact myself as an adult whilst in training. I felt great empathy towards both my parents as I learned all about psychological theories and realized that they did their best in whatever way they could. They were limited in their capacity to offer what I needed due to their own traumatic upbringings. As old-fashioned parents, they never looked inwards or undertook any form of therapy; their way was to autopilot through life, ignoring their misery.

My parents were not self-aware, and they lived and died in that state, which saddens me to this day. The saying goes, 'what you do not heal you repeat', which is why as a social worker I saw generations of families coming into the care system over the years, from grandparents to grandchildren, all within the same family and unable to break the toxic negative cycle of abuse.

As a parent myself, I have broken that cycle and learned how to develop my self-awareness, I flipped the script and created my own narrative no longer blindly or subconsciously following in parental footsteps. I celebrate every small victory and achievement my children have. I hug and kiss my children and tell them often that I love them and am proud of them. (This did not happen in my childhood family home growing up.)

I feed them with positivity, and this has helped me to heal as an adult. We all carry within ourselves our child selves who may need healing due to childhood traumas or abuse suffered. This is why therapeutic intervention is so important; through counselling, we can unpick our past hurts and unresolved pain and begin the healing process. We need to recognize and separate our parents' emotional baggage from our own and give to ourselves the validation that was not given to us by them when we needed it.

The saying 'trying to get blood from a stone' comes to mind. Often, they don't have it to give it or don't know how to give us what we need because of their own history and upbringing. After chasing approval for so long, we can become numb to it. The good news is YOU can break the cycle and heal yourself by accepting that, despite their efforts, your parents may never be your validators. As such, we need to become our own champions and cheerleaders, our own validators and our own source of peace.

I won't lie to you: it can be a painful journey of self-discovery, but therapy is worth every step because of the amount of burden that is lifted from addressing, processing and releasing past trauma and stuck emotions. It also paves the way forward for you to become the best version of yourself according to who you want to be. Not dictated by others or your past. Once you identify, address and work on your own triggers, defences, coping mechanisms and behaviours, you can master the art of being you. Nobody else but you, and that is enough. You will learn to accept and believe in yourself and that, my dear readers…that will bring you peace.

Exercise:

Now, try and think back to your own childhoods:

- What negative or positive messages did you receive? Feel free to list them in your journal to explore as you read further.
- How have they impacted your life today? Feel free to journal or reflect on how your past has impacted your present.
- Do you still believe those comments to be true? Have others' views of you cemented in your mind and become a self-fulfilling prophecy?
- Or, have you flipped the script and created your own reality in which such negative comments that caused pain have now been harnessed into powerful ways of helping yourself and others?
- Through self-awareness, have you been able to challenge those perceptions and remove others' negative views from your heart and mind, replacing them with kinder beliefs that you own?

Often, self-image is developed by recognizing how others are perceiving us. We then become consciously aware of the 'other' and try to put ourselves in their shoes. We try and think about how they view events or situations playing out. This is called 'imitation' of a role, known as the 'generalized other'. By taking on the role of the other, we can become self-aware and develop a sense of empathy. As we become more aware of ourselves, we develop two parts of the self.

1. Self-image: The idea one has of one's abilities, appearance, and personality.

2. Self-awareness: Conscious knowledge of one's own character and feelings.

To illustrate this point, picture this scene:

Children are playing together in a nursery playground where there is a 'Play House' and dress up toy box full of outfits. Some children begin to role play 'doctors and nurses'; others play 'mummies and daddies' assigning roles of the mum, dad and child and enacting those roles in what they have seen at home (self-images in play). Stereotypically, children may enact mummy busy cooking in the kitchen and daddy going to work with baby crying for attention (although in many families, this can be quite different).

Young children reflect back their lived experience of the world around them in the purest sense as they have no filters. They take on the generalised role of the other from watching adults around them— children live what they learn. Children are not self-aware enough to know the difference between the 'Me' or 'I' yet.

It could be quite amusing to watch a diverse group of young children play mummies and daddies together from very different backgrounds, maybe where mummy works and daddy stays at home or single parent families, then watch the ensuing confusion between the children whose parents live different lifestyles. Each child may believe their way is the right way because it's what they see at home.

Ultimately, children copy or 'imitate' what they see, then gradually learn to take the point of view of several significant adults in their lives, often simultaneously. Then finally, when they are fully socialized, they take on the viewpoint of society in general. This happens when people have internalized the widespread cultural norms and expectations of what is acceptable behaviour in that society.

Exercise:

Now, consider your own behaviour:

- How have you been shaped by the others?
- And how do you think others view you and your behaviour?

In summary of this chapter, we have the 'I' part of the self and the 'Me' part of the self.

The 'I' part is the part of you that's inherently inside you—your natural self, being spontaneous and doing things in the world. It is the subject of action. It's what you would probably commonly think of as your authentic self. The 'Me' is the person you present to the outside world combined with the image of yourself that has been given to you from others while interacting with society.

'Me' is basically the part of you that society sees, one of the versions of yourself that you feel safe to show off to the world in any given situation.

For example, the 'Me' would expect to go straight into a job right after finishing studies, because that is what society expects, but the 'I' might respond and say, *"Actually, I just want to rest and relax for a year or travel a bit before I start working."* 'Me' is the part that does things that are in keeping with society's expectations. 'I' is more spontaneous in terms of its actions, and less likely to conform to society's norms. To break it down further, the concept of 'Me' enables the individual to regulate the behaviour of 'I', which can be impulsive.

"The relationship you have with yourself sets the tone for every other relationship you will ever have." (Robert Holden)

Chapter 2

The Practical Understanding

I want you now to consider that when you interact with people, what might they be thinking of you? What judgments, assumptions, stereotypes or biases might they hold from communicating with you, based on how you look, speak, and present? Then, I would like you to reflect on your own view of yourself. Process your thoughts about this for a moment.

Exercise:

- What are your core values?
- Who do you think you are?
- What do you think other people think of you?
- Do you know what your personality is?
- Do you consciously filter what you show others?

Try to recall recent conversations you have had with people. They may have said something to you, like, "*Oh, that was really clever,*" or, "*That was amazing,*" or, "*That was really stupid*".

How did those comments make you feel about yourself? It's precisely this point that Mead is getting at, which is why we can benefit from this theory.

"*A deep sense of love and belonging is an irreducible need of all people. We are biologically, cognitively, physically, and spiritually wired to love, to be loved, and to belong. When those needs are not met, we don't function as we were meant to. We break. We fall apart. We numb. We ache. We hurt others. We get sick."*

(Brene Brown)

This is a particularly interesting theory of the self because it is entirely social. Consider for a moment that a child doesn't have any interaction with society. They are only their true biological self. Imagine a Mowgli type from The Jungle book—raised by wolves, he acts like a wolf in a pack and not as a human, simply because of how he was raised and socialised. Everything that makes us human is given to us in social interaction. We are but a collection of people living in relation to the other.

Theoretically, the ideal is a person who has a 'definite personality', who thinks for themselves, is acutely self-aware and can think outside the box, not an automatic conformist but one who replies to the organized attitude in a way that makes a significant difference. With such a person, the *'I'* is the most important part of the experience but a healthy combination of the 'I' and 'Me' in balance are required to fully form a personality. These types of people are more in tune with themselves and are able to live more fulfilling lives to achieve their true potential in life by living as their authentic selves.

Remember the 'Me' is what is learned in social interaction with others and once other people's attitudes and beliefs about who you are have been internalised into yourself, it becomes the 'Me' you believe yourself to be.

"What the individual is for himself is not something that he invented. It is what his significant others have come to …treat him as being." (George Herbert Mead)

"It is only after we have acted that we know what we have done...what we have said. The "I" reacts to the self which arises through the taking of the attitude of others." (George Herbert Mead)

The 'Me' disciplines the 'I' by holding it back from breaking the law of the land. The 'I' acts creatively, on impulse but within the context of the 'Me', and does not blindly follow rules. They develop a response on the basis of what they have learned, through the 'Me'. Mead explained that both the 'I' and 'Me' need to be taken together to form a whole in his social philosophy; there would be no possibility of personality without both the 'I' and the 'Me'.

Okay, now that we have established the theory, let's start some exercises that will help you fully understand and appreciate this concept and apply it in practice to your life. Let's begin by exploring who YOU see yourself as in each of these phases.

Exercise:

Who is the 'I' and who is the 'Me'?

To start you off, an example of 'I' could be, "I feel afraid of mixing in big crowds; it's nerve-wracking and I never know what to say." (Vulnerability, rawness, honesty.)

An example of 'Me' could be, "I always dress smart so that people assume I am clever and know what I am talking about, even when I don't." (Social mask; trying to appear a certain way to fit in or be accepted.)

List the 'I' attributes here: (Remember, 'I' is your authentic self who you really are, without masks; just you and what you think of yourself)

_____

_____

_____

_____

_____

_____

Now, list the 'Me' attributes to your personality: (The part that is socialised, who you are to the outside world; your social mask that you present to other people)

_____

_____

_____

_____

_____

_____

Note: You may find that both lists have similarities as you are sharing thoughts on who you are internally and externally. What I want you to focus on are the differences in both lists—that's where the personal development areas are, the areas to reflect on more and challenge or change if you so wish.

The routines that you have developed through your life have been learned by heart so that most of the time, you don't even need to think about what you are doing; it's on autopilot. The thing to remember is that it doesn't matter what others think, as long as you are happy with what you do or say and as long as it is within the law and doesn't hurt anyone else.

It is what you believe about yourself that counts—you are in charge of deciding who you want to be, not anybody else. If you are happy and satisfied that you are doing the right thing, the opinions of others are just that—their opinions. They are entitled to their own thoughts and views, just as you are to yours. What you must acknowledge is that it is impossible to please all people all of the time and everyone makes mistakes now and again. Accept that no one is perfect and allow for everyone to live life each to their own.

"I have done my best. That is all the philosophy of living one needs." (Lin-Yutang)

"You're imperfect, and you're wired for struggle, but you are worthy of love and belonging." (Brene Brown)

Chapter 3

Identity Loss

?*Who am I?*

Having discussed what the 'I in Me' signifies and worked with this on a theoretical level, we must establish who we are in practice. This can become a challenge if we do not have a clear identity or view of ourselves or if we are going through an identity crisis.

How do you 'lose' your identity?

Losing your identity can be a long process that occurs over a period of months or years, but it can also happen suddenly following a major life event or trauma. Loss of identity can impact every area of our lives, both personally and professionally. The loss of a job or profession or the loss of a significant loved one, such as a child, parent, or spouse can devastate us. Loss leaves gaps, empty spaces. Such losses can trigger increased levels of anxiety, low self-worth, depression, isolation and feelings of loneliness, all of which impact on our ability to maintain relationships with other people.

Identity can also be lost when entering into a relationship that becomes imbalanced. A healthy relationship offers both partners the opportunity to connect with one another without cutting off the outside world. It promotes reciprocation in respecting the other and maintaining an individual sense of self. It is important, however, to make compromises, even in the healthiest of relationships, as we try to adjust our behaviours and accommodate our partners to create a dynamic that works for the relationship.

However, in abusive relationships, this change could be more obvious, resulting in one partner dominating the other and removing choice, control and independence, causing a total loss of who you are. This can often be seen in families where domestic abuse has become 'normalised' via systematic conditioning over time. Often, when we lose our identity and sense of who we are, we look to others for our sense of self-worth, needing external validation and fulfilment.

We feel the need to seek reassurance from others and what they think of us shapes how we view ourselves. We glean our self-esteem, confidence and self-worth from others based on how they perceive us according to factors like how we dress, our physical appearance and financial status. We seek praise from others to feel 'OK' about ourselves—but in reality, our emotional well-being depends on how we feel about ourselves and not what others think of us.

Exercise:

1.   At the core of yourself do you like, accept, value and respect who you are and what you stand for?

2.   If not, why?

What are your Core Beliefs?

We all have certain core beliefs; some are positive, but many are negative and may cause harmful consequences. In order to challenge your negative core beliefs, you first need to identify what they are. Here are some common examples:

"I'm unlovable"

"I'm boring"

"I'm not good enough"

"I'm ugly"

"I'm worthless"

Exercise: What are your negative core beliefs?

Once you have listed them, I want you to follow it up with pieces of evidence contrary to each negative core belief.

For example, "I'm not good enough." — "Actually, despite all the hardships I have faced so far in my life I am still standing and have made good friends, have loving family members and have managed to find a good job."

Our self-worth or our 'identity' can be informed by our own experiences of self and not from what others think about us. Too often we worry about others judging us and we put way too much emphasis on how we look, or behave in order to 'fit in', be accepted and be liked. What we forget is that others have their own stuff going on, too. Each person is waging a war with their own selves and could be projecting their own insecurities onto others. Hence, when being measured by others, we often fall short of their requirements and

27

expectations—so what do we do? We act, we become the big pretenders, creating an illusion of self that seems more acceptable…but wearing this mask can become exhausting.

We hide the real 'me' underneath layers of social masks, afraid of rejection or of not being good enough if we show our true selves. What if I'm not funny enough, or likeable enough or clever enough to hang out with this or that group?

It can become problematic when this is happening all the time, when we are more our 'created selves' than our 'genuine selves'. It can divide the psyche, causing inner conflict and confusion between what we say, what we do and how we think. Such contradictions can lead to personal anxiety and unhappiness. Our continued dependency on others for validation prevents our true selves from being out there and impacts our personal growth, as well as the opportunity for happiness. Our life experiences shape who we have become and often, by looking at the past, we can track our life changes and see what led us to who we are today. Suffice to say nobody was born anxious or with the complex personality issues they develop via socialisation.

To explore this further, meet 'Donna'—she was bullied at school by peers and had abusive parents at home who would argue all the time. As a result, she developed anger issues as a defence to cope with life and suffered with low self-esteem into adulthood because her childhood issues were left unresolved. Parental neglect, abuse and trauma from childhood impacted how Donna viewed herself; she found herself repeating the cycle with a string of failed relationships. Her blueprint for life came from a dysfunctional and emotionally unhealthy home.

Donna learned through watching her parents how to be; violence and abuse were normalised in her upbringing. In her romantic relationships, she found herself drawn to dominant and abusive men but would feel trapped, and this then triggered an emotional response to past memories of her violent parental relationship, causing her to regress back to that childhood state of being fearful and anxious as the associated feelings became overwhelming. This would result in Donna running away when things got really bad.

This is not to assume that all children from abusive homes grow up to repeat the cycle. This is just a typical example of how years of conditioning can impact our personalities when we are not self-aware. Many of us do grow up and break the cycle through seeking out loving, healthy partners or via therapy and self-help literature.

We all share in common a longing for acceptance and reassurance from others; to be noticed, to be loved, to be seen, wanted and needed, to be cared about. What if we could offer all of those things to ourselves? How amazing would that be? Imagine feeling okay to show everyone our true selves and not be afraid? It may be a challenge but with the right support, determination and an open outlook, such things can be achieved. It all begins with trust; if you can learn to trust in yourself, listen to yourself, have self-compassion, and value who you are then it's all good.

We often hear how important maintaining a sense of well-being is, but what does that actually mean in practice?

What factors contribute to feeling well?

The following are important factors in promoting good emotional health and well-being.

- Good family relationships
- A manageable financial situation
- A positive work environment
- Community engagement and a good social network of friends, family and work colleagues.
- Health: this covers good physical health via eating well, exercising and sleeping enough. Emotional and psychological health via expressing emotions freely amongst trusted friends and family or via a therapist. Self-awareness, self-acceptance and valuing oneself. Spiritual health for those who like to feel connected with universal energies, be that via God / organised religion or a belief in nature and appreciation for humanity at its best.
- Personal freedom: Feeling strong, empowered, liberated and in control of one's life.
- Personal values: knowing oneself, identifying what's important and striving to achieve it.
- Resilience and patience to bear with life's challenges
- Continuing to stimulate the brain intellectually by learning new things to enhance and enrich your life.

Realistically, how many of us can say that we have all of the above in place? It's inevitable that we will all face challenges in life at one time or another, so it's about how we cope and manage with the support we do or don't have that counts.

Looking at the list above, it is clear that the polar opposite of those descriptions could result in depression, anxiety and mental ill-health. Problems can develop and be perpetuated in an ongoing cycle causing distress, trauma, fear and a sense of helplessness. Therefore, understanding a person's past and present life in a fuller context by taking into account the above-listed factors can help make sense of how and why people may feel the way they do. This in turn will help to identify appropriate support mechanisms.

In order to promote a healthy sense of well-being, we need to continue to develop as individuals. We must ask for help from others when we need it—forge stronger bonds and connect with others in the community, not just online in the virtual world but in real life, socialising with people directly.

It is important that we learn more about ourselves and others. This will increase our self-awareness and enable us to identify our own needs, desires, defences and vulnerabilities. How can we help ourselves if we don't truly understand who we are? Ongoing personal development is the deal of the day…it will provide valuable insights and stimulate the winds of change that you want to see in your life. One key point to remember is that we can only really control and change ourselves, not others. Our power lies in what we think, say, do, act and how we react to others.

I can't control
Anyone else
But I can control
Myself

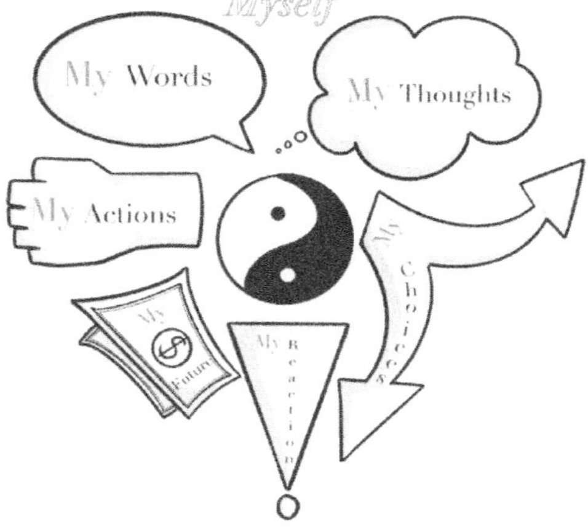

Chapter 4
Worksheets

Now this book would not be complete without some coping tools that you can use in your daily life to help you become more self-aware, calm and in control. The following pages are activities you can undertake yourself to help you become more authentically you and worry less about the 'what if's' in life.

To begin with, it may be helpful to practice some mindfulness techniques to encourage calm and a natural slowing down process. I would like you to read and follow the instructions offered below to get into a relaxed meditative state so that you are ready to complete the tasks ahead that require focus and attention. This exercise should take no longer than around 10-15 minutes. It's called the 'Body Scan'. Try to do this activity at least once a day in the morning or evening when you have time; if not daily, at least once a week during a quiet period so you can touch base with yourself and recalibrate.

*"Crazy-busy' is a great armour, it's a great way for numbing. What a lot of us do is that we stay so busy, and so out in front of our life, that the truth of how we're feeling and what we really need can't catch up with us." (*Brene Brown*)

Body Scan Meditation

To get maximum benefit, read the following script out loud and record your voice so you can listen to it anytime.

Find a place where you can sit in peace and quiet without any distractions for a few moments. I want you to start by bringing your attention to your breathing. Notice its rhythmic nature as you inhale in and exhale out; notice how your chest rises and falls with each breath. Take your time and gradually slow down your breathing by inhaling and exhaling for longer. Now, focus your mind on the present moment by focusing solely on your breathing for a few minutes.

Allow for whatever background noises are happening. Tune them out and start noticing how your mind starts drifting to random thoughts distracting you from this moment—don't worry; that is normal, so allow it. Try to imagine stepping outside of yourself and notice what thoughts and feelings you are having in your mind. Make a mental note of this and re-focus on your breathing; imagine inhaling a white, pure energy and exhaling dark clouds of worry and stress. Let go…breathe out all that negativity. Close your eyes at this point and drop your shoulders, loosen your limbs and just practice this breathing for a few moments.

Okay, now open your eyes and notice where your thoughts are going, then accept what's happening. Now, focus your awareness to the physical sensations in your body, especially to the sensations of touch or pressure, where your body is making contact with the chair, sofa or bed.

On each breath out allow yourself to let go, sinking a little deeper into your seat. Bring your awareness to any sensations you detect, as you focus your attention on each part of your body in turn. Start with any physical sensations you feel around your face, head and neck. Notice any tension and allow your facial muscles to relax and your eyebrows to relax; no frowning. Let your jaw relax without clenching and allow your neck and shoulders to relax. As you move down to your upper arms and into your elbows and hands, notice any tension and relax them. Relax your hands, no fists, and let your hands rest and sit comfortably on your sides or on your knees.

Now, move to your chest area and abdomen; feel the flutter of your heart and notice then how your abdomen rises and falls with every breath. If you feel any tension, try to relax the area and breathe away the tension. Become aware of the changing patterns of sensations in the abdominal wall as you breathe in and as you breathe out. Having connected with the sensations in the abdomen, bring the focus of your awareness down to your right leg, into your right foot, and out of your toes on your right foot.

Focus on each of the toes of your right foot in turn, exploring the feelings and sensations you may be feeling in your toes. Perhaps a sense of tingling or cool air, or no particular sensation at all. Now focus on your left leg, into your left foot and out of your left toes. Feel for any sensations in this area before moving on to the next part.

When you are ready, inhale deeply and feel your lungs fill up, the air going up from your nose into your abdomen, and then as you exhale feel your breath come up through the abdomen in to your nose and out of your mouth as you release that air. Try this for a few breaths and focus on your body as it inhales good energy and exhales bad energy. Now, allow this body awareness to expand into the rest of yourself.

Visualise the air you breathe in as a ball of white light energy that moves its way through your body beginning from the top of your head to the tips of your toes. Feel the energy you breathe in flow from your head down to your throat—into your stomach—down through your legs—and out through your toes as you exhale. Continue to bring awareness, and a gentle curiosity, to the physical sensations in each part of the rest of the body in turn. Remember to scan every part of your body including your upper and lower back and pelvic area.

In each area, as best you can, bring the same detailed level of awareness and gentle curiosity to the bodily sensations present.

After you have "scanned" the whole body in this way, spend a few minutes being aware of a sense of the body as a whole, and of each of your breaths flowing freely in and out of the body. You may find you are relaxed and sleepy after this exercise, so allow yourself a quick nap, if possible, for rest.

Soul-Searching Questions

Have a think about the following questions, and then write down your answers on a separate sheet of paper.

- Who am I to me?
- What makes me who I am?
- Who am I to others?
- Do I like me?
- Do others like me?
- What do I think of myself?
- Do others' perceptions of me match my own views of who I am?
- Who is the real me no masks?
- Who is the 'me' I show to the world?
- Who is the 'me' I hide out of fear, guilt, shame, embarrassment or just plain secrecy?
- Who is the 'me' I pretend to be?
- Who is the 'me' I would like to be?
- What does being me mean to myself and others?
- What parts of me do I like, and why?
- What parts of me do I dislike, and why?
- Who was I before (past self)?
- Who am I now (present self)?
- Who do I want to be (future self)?

"The truth is: Belonging starts with self-acceptance. Your level of belonging, in fact, can never be greater than your level of self-acceptance, because believing that you're enough is what gives you the courage to be authentic, vulnerable and imperfect." (Brene Brown)

What Are Your Values?

To get to know yourself better, it helps to question what you value in life and who influenced these decisions. Notice how your values may have changed over the years with life experiences.

Exercise:

1.   List your mother's values

2.   List your father's values

3.   List the values of a person that you respect or admire

4.   List the values you would like to live by

5.   List the values you actually live by

Notice how many of your values overlap with those of your parents and what values are missing from your list that you like about your respected person. Start working on your own values and reflect on how you can incorporate the missing desired values into your lifestyle.

Me Map

For the next exercise, I want you to brainstorm your worries in list form or as a spider graph and then number them in order of priority. Below is an example of a Me Map to illustrate the different aspects of your life to consider.

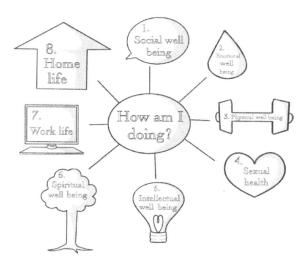

The above figure is the 'Me Map'. It details every aspect of your life and helps you reflect on what is happening in your life right now; it gets you to think about how you are feeling.

Sometimes we need to stop, think and reflect before we can make positive changes in our lives. Just like a jigsaw puzzle, it helps to take everything apart and put it back together again but in the correct order for you. Getting the right balance in life can be quite difficult and, often, we struggle. Using the 'Me Map', you can begin to unpick what is happening and sort through what is important and how we can achieve a happier, more fulfilled life.

What are you waiting for? Get cracking and draw or list your own areas to work on. See if you can identify what you need to address about your life. What needs your immediate attention, and what can wait?

1.

2.

3.

4.

5.

6.

7.

8.

This frees up headspace and helps to organise thoughts to reduce the clutter of the mind when life feels so full.

The Life-Changing Miracle Question

Okay, so now that you have identified the top priorities in life you need to address you have a clearer picture of what to tackle first so you can address the changes needed to make it a reality. Be proactive and start to plan ahead on how you intend to improve matters. Use the question below to start planning:

Exercise:

Q: If you woke up tomorrow and your life was amazing, exactly how you want it to be, what would it look like? (Be as realistic as possible.)

- What would have changed?
- How would it have changed?
- How can you make that change a reality?
- How would you behave differently?
- How would you treat others differently?
- How would you treat yourself differently?
- What sorts of things would you start doing?
- What would you stop doing?
- What goals would you set and work towards?
- Now, list the steps needed to make it true- how will you achieve this, be precise exactly what will you do, and by when.

The Line of Control

The next tool will help you in recognising limitations to control outside of yourself and help you to stop self-sabotaging, being a perfectionist or setting impossible standards for yourself. As you are aware, you can control yourself but not others.

For this next exercise, I need you to visualise a clean white sheet of paper. Next, imagine taking a thick, black permanent marker and drawing a line horizontally across the length of the paper so it's now in two halves. "***What is above the line is what is in your control... What is below the line is NOT in your control***". To illustrate this, I will use the following example:

Claire's mother became ill suddenly and was hospitalised, however, Claire felt responsible because she had not visited that particular week and believes if she had she could have prevented this from happening.

- Claire's mother falling ill = Below the line; it was never in Claire or anybody else's control.
- Claire's emotional response of feeling responsible = Above the line; it's what is in her control, how she responded to the situation.

The point is that we have limited control over some things in life and with those things we have to have radical acceptance—there's nothing we could have done about it. This then alleviates the burden of guilt or responsibility and accountability on oneself as there was nothing they could do to prevent that thing from happening. So, why stress, worry or remove your peace of mind for something you can't control?

Now, what is above the line is what you CAN do in respect of the situation. It's how you react and respond to the situation. It's what IS in your control, and you can do something about it.

So in the above example Claire is worrying and feeling responsible for something that was never in her control. Even if she had visited her mother, the illness was already in her mother's system and could not be prevented. Therefore, if Claire applied this concept to her situation, she would see that her mother's illness was never within her control and could therefore alleviate some of the guilt she is feeling. What she CAN do about the situation moving forwards—what is above the line is what is in her control. She could plan more visits to see her mother in the future, and make more regular phone calls to check up on her, hire home help so that she is being monitored regularly, etc.

This would afford Claire a greater sense of control over what she can do to support her mother moving forwards. Also, it would help her to accept that in life, some things are beyond her control so to worry about them is fruitless and stress-inducing, making her more susceptible to negative thoughts about herself, which would only compound the matter. Instead, she can learn to accept the situation as it is, recognise her own limitations and react and respond in the most appropriate way to help, and not blame herself for matters beyond her control. You see the difference?

This concept of understanding what is and is not in your control can be applied to any area of your life. It can help to unburden many a worry and allow for clarity and control in your response. So, in your next crisis, remember this method; it will surely help you to be calmer, more measured and accepting in your response.

"Daring to set boundaries is about having the courage to love ourselves, even when we risk disappointing others". (Brene Brown)

Try to practice using this method for a current situation of your own on the blank worksheet below:

The Marker of Control

What IS in your control- what you can do about the situation- how you react and respond.

The Line of
Control

What is NOT in your control- fate/destiny/accidents/
other people.

The Mental Filter Funnel

This next worksheet requires some focus from you in respect to thought processing. I need you to visualise a funnel with two halves (see below for an illustration).

This is what I call the Mental Filter Funnel; it works by filtering out negative thoughts and comments internally from yourself and externally by others through the colon, into the wastepipes and out, whilst retaining positive thoughts and comments from yourself internally and others outside of you to your heart. Both positive and negative comments enter the funnel of your mind but are filtered to their correct place by you.

Consider what you would write into your funnel—what positives would you retain, and which negatives would you expel?

Remember, this activity includes your own thoughts as well as remarks others have made to you. The beauty of this funnel is that YOU are in control of it. All you need to do is visualise bad words out and good words in. Positive thoughts in and negative thoughts out. Filtering can take some getting used to, which is why using visual aids like the mental filter funnel can help.

Mental filter funnel

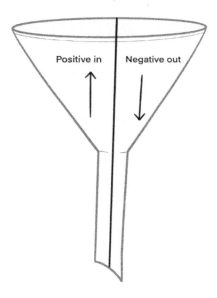

"What's the greater risk? Letting go of what people think - or letting go of how I feel, what I believe, and who I am?" (Brene Brown)

The Invisible Teflon Armour Suit

In keeping with the above technique, I also developed the idea of an **Invisible Teflon Armour Suit** that you can imagine wearing when feeling attacked or insulted verbally by others. This one works well with young people and adults alike.

Similar to superheroes like Spiderman or Batman, who wear their outfits as a defence against dark forces to protect them, this concept is in keeping with that theme. Imagine the next time somebody says something hurtful to you, instead of internalising it or believing it to be true—recognise it is just their opinion and their words and not your reality.

You can literally switch on and power up your Armour suit so that none of their words hurt you—they literally slide off of you like those non-stick cooking pans. None of their words stick to you.

They can't get past your suit and penetrate your heart or mind. You will be safe from their harsh words and can choose to ignore them. No longer will you internalise other people's negative views about you.

The great thing about this suit is you get to design it and visualise how it will look and fit, what colours it contains and any special design features it has for additional security and support.

Here's an image to get your creative juices flowing:

*Without the suit on, mentally you are vulnerable to harsh words and can be broken more easily like the figure on the left. With the suit on you are powerful and protected, safe from the cruel words of others; it's all in your mind-set, so visualise yours now.

Have a go at designing your own suit and remember to add any additional features.

"When you get to a place where you understand that love and belonging, your worthiness, is a birth-right and not something you have to earn, anything is possible." (Brene Brown)

Freeze Frame

My next tip is the 'Freeze Frame' technique. Imagine you could pause time for a second and think of the consequences of your words, thoughts and actions, then consider:

- What are my options here?
- What's the worst that could happen if I took a certain course of action?
- What are the positives of taking a certain course of action?
- Almost like the traffic light system stop/look/listen, only in this you pause, think, and act.

This helps to limit over analysing things and ending up thinking the worst-case scenario and encourages considering options in a more balanced way. So, the next time you are conflicted about what decision to make, think through the situation using the above set of questions. Don't act in haste or make any snap decisions. Remember the old adage, 'act in haste repent at leisure'.

If it helps, write down your answers—or think them through in your head. Either way, this will help you clarify things. Keeping a journal or diary of your thoughts can help, so if you enjoy writing it will assist the therapeutic process by supporting you in tracking your own progress.

To help you formulate your own freeze frame, I have added an example of one below with the prompts included to practice when considering tough decisions or trying to prevent hasty ones.

Remember, this technique can be used in any real-life scenario and be effective. It's a thought process tool that allows for balanced thinking.

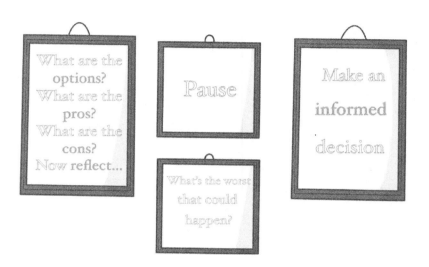

"*Perfectionism is not the same thing as striving to be our best. Perfectionism is not about healthy achievement and growth; it's a shield.*" (Brene Brown*)*

Now that you have completed some of the activities illustrated above, you will be more self-aware and have a better idea of who you are. Next, we can tackle the issue of authenticity and who you present to the outside world. If the two are very different, there may be an inner conflict about your identity.

To illustrate this point, see the diagram below:

Authentic Me

Authentic me 'I'

Socially constructed 'Me'

To become the most authentic version of yourself, the two figures above would ideally merge into one, or at least be closer together. The distance between the two pictured above is quite vast, indicating this subject could be having an identity crisis, presenting as one person to the outside world but being quite different behind closed doors when alone. To be true to yourself and minimise emotional conflict within the self, it is important to note how far you feel from your authentic self. There is a spectrum, a scale if you like, and we all slide up and down that scale at different times of our lives as we grow and develop.

The closer together each part of you is to the other, the more healthy, whole and yourself you will feel.

Do you feel you can be yourself in public as you are in private? Notwithstanding context, of course—for example at work, there is an expectation to maintain professional boundaries—but do you change so much that you almost morph into a different personality in different scenarios? I call this 'social chameleoning' where you change your social skin, metaphorically speaking, in each setting around individuals or groups so much so that if the two groups met, they would describe you very differently.

Or, do you have constancy in your personality wherever you go and whomever you are with? I understand it is necessary to wear different hats or masks, if you like, when in different roles professionally, but do you do the same with friends and family? How much of your personality do you filter and around whom? Who do you feel you can truly be yourself around?

If the answer to that is nobody…then there is much work to do around developing your identity boosting self-esteem and becoming more self-accepting. There is a reason you feel this way and often it is connected to your past experiences in life of being yourself around others who have not approved of or accepted you, which has caused you to doubt yourself. Remember, other people's opinions of you are just that—opinions—and the solution is to be happy in yourself with who you are.

Granted, nobody likes to be disliked by others, hence the reason why we constantly seek approval from others externally, particularly as young children. However, there has to come a point in your life when other people's views no longer overshadow your own and you start to live life according to your own values and beliefs and stop comparing your life to others. The need to belong and feel accepted in society is great, but the need for self-acceptance must be greater for if you do not accept yourself, how can you expect others to?

Fulfilling your own expectations of yourself is something to focus on primarily to create a sense of purpose and meaning in your life. To have an identity you can be proud of and accept as uniquely yours. Nobody else in this world has walked in your shoes and experienced life through your eyes, so that in itself makes the task very personal to you. Only you can help yourself to get to where you are going in life and unblock your mind and heart to the potential you have. Sometimes, however, we all struggle due to our inner dialogue. In the next chapter, I will highlight some of those issues and how to manage those negative, self-limiting beliefs that keep you in a dark place.

Chapter 5

Core Issues

Conquering the Assassin Within

Have you ever wondered why sometimes you just can't get that critical voice out of your head? You know…the one that tells you how useless you are and how you will never get anywhere in life?

Somebody once described it as having their own inner assassin that would murder any positive thoughts he had and replace them with doubt and fear of failure. This would prevent him from trying new things and forming new relationships. So, who is this assassin, and what are they repeatedly whispering to you?

We have already examined what we think of ourselves, and to recap, as young children we are hugely influenced by the significant adults around us and what they say has a lot of value and weight. If you grew up being told you were stupid, ugly and useless by significant people around you, chances are they formed part of your critical inner voice as you internalised those negative views. Often, our critical inner voice is mistaken for our own conscience, but it is not—the difference is our conscience is a moral guide. It doesn't bully us, it reasons with us. The critical inner voice is always negative, hurtful, defensive and cruel to us.

It is the part of us that is turned against ourselves, the negative part of our personality that is against our personal development. The voice is highly judgmental and encourages self-defeatist thoughts and behaviours. It revels in making us feel unworthy, unloved and to have low self-esteem. It sneers at us and sows seeds of doubt in our capabilities, encouraging us to have a cynical and pessimistic view of the world around us and teaching us not to trust others; it keeps us in a state of conflict, anxiety and disharmony. We all struggle with our critical inner voice to varying degrees but if we "listen" to its destructive points of view and actually believe what it is saying to us, then we will fail to challenge it. Instead, we will act on it with seriously negative consequences on our lives.

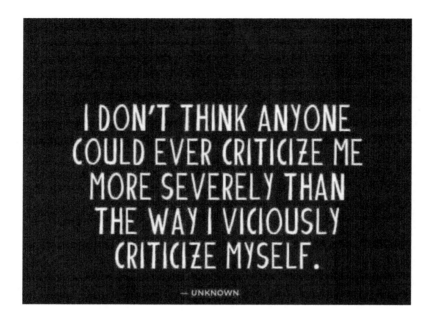

I DON'T THINK ANYONE COULD EVER CRITICIZE ME MORE SEVERELY THAN THE WAY I VICIOUSLY CRITICIZE MYSELF.

— UNKNOWN

So, how can you challenge your critical inner voice? You can take back your power when you become conscious of what it is telling you. Self- awareness is key here; know yourself enough to understand when the voice is destructive so you can stop it from running your life. The challenge is to identify and eliminate this toxic internal dialogue. To do this, be mindful around times of sudden mood changes, upset and anger. Think about what caused this shift, what triggered this reaction and, most importantly, what did you start telling yourself after the event? The fact that your mood shifted from feeling positive or relaxed to feeling upset or frustrated is probably an indication that you are interpreting the event via your critical inner voice.

Once you have identified that it is your critical inner voice that is advising you, reflect on what it wants you to do. If those actions would cause pain, hurt, upset or destruction, then understand that you have a choice to **not** act on those instructions; instead, take control over your critical inner voice. You can consciously decide to take action against its suggestions and do what feels right and better for you and your personal development. It's about catching the thought as it tries to embed itself and change it from a negative action towards a more positive goal, acting in your own best interests.

For example: you are about to go out on a date; you look in the mirror and your critical inner voice pipes up, "*You look awful—you can't go out wearing that. Nothing looks good on you, and anyway, who would look twice at you? Once they get to know the real you they will dump you anyway. Don't even bother trying; it's not worth it.*"

Imagine that is you—what would you do next? Could you recognise that was your critical inner voice or would you succumb to its toxic whispers?

Remember that you **do** have a choice and can **choose** not to be controlled by it; just take your time and have some self-compassion and patience to slowly undo those years of conditioning to become the person **you** want to be. Repeat to yourself either in the mirror or out loud that you are better than the thoughts you are having. Remind yourself that they are just thoughts and not reality. Challenge your inner critic.

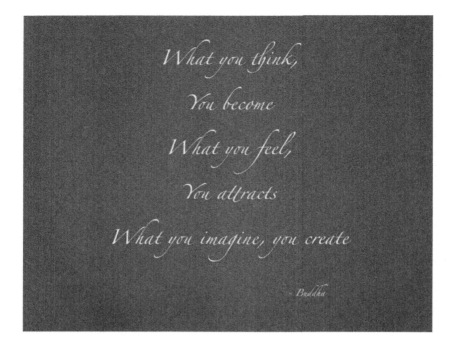

What you think,
You become
What you feel,
You attracts
What you imagine, you create

– Buddha

One way is to imagine a close friend or family member being in the same predicament and confiding in you that they feel ugly, horrible and worthless. What would you say to them? I can guarantee you would not bully them further or allow them to sit with such awful thoughts about themselves. Most likely you would show compassion and love and offer caring and reassuring words of kindness to support and uplift their spirits. So, if you can do this for someone else, then please do it for yourself. Why is it okay to be kind to others yet bully your own souls? That is unjust and oppressive. Become your own champion against those critical inner voices.

Self-Sabotage

As a counsellor, the amount of people I see in my therapy room with a harsh inner critic that will not allow them to be free is quite astounding. So many of us have such limiting beliefs about ourselves which keep us chained up internally from progressing forwards. Fear of failure, dislike of ourselves, feeling unloved or unworthy and not trusting in our own judgment have left many emotionally exhausted and unhappy. It doesn't need to be like this. The past does not have to repeat in the future and any current issues can be managed with the right support.

If you feel you need that additional support then don't be afraid to look up a local counsellor and get the help you need. This book is useful as a tool but sometimes you need that bit of extra practical help to feel more supported.

If we look at the cause of much of our unhappiness, it's often in the mind-set and thought processes we have. We may over analyse, self-depreciate and self-sabotage as a coping mechanism or defence. It may be learnt behaviour we saw as young children and picked up from parents and other significant adults in our lives. After all, they do say our first teachers are our parents; therefore, if they had depression, anxiety or suffered with low self-esteem, chances are you picked up on this as a child and have learnt similar behaviours or coping mechanisms.

There are several ways to combat self-sabotage—the following are some points to reflect on:

- Do you feel unloved and therefore strive for perfection to hide this feeling? What pressure does that place on you?
- Do you feel broken because of past events and feel the need to hide this and appear whole? Does this cause you inner conflict and exhaustion?
- Do you have a fear of failure? Explore where this came from and how it stops you from progressing in life.
- Do you feel guilt and therefore feel you need to be punished? If so, are you in fact punishing yourself? And what memory or thought is linked to this guilt?
- What goals or ambitions in life have you been unable to achieve?
- Try to identify the behaviours and triggers that are stopping you from achieving your goals.
- Do you feel shame and hide or suppress your desires as a result? What is it that causes you to feel this way?

- Do you feel blame for everything that goes wrong and therefore you need to be carrying the world on your shoulders?
- Do you procrastinate over even the smallest task?

Proactive Pointers:

- Make a note of your negative thoughts when you are next feeling low and then evaluate the list; is there anything you can do to resolve any of the items listed?
- Looking at the list, go through each point and challenge yourself on these thoughts—what is your evidence base? How can you justify them?
- Start to action plan how you intend to achieve your goals. Start organising yourself and set yourself small tasks each day to chunk it out so it's not so overwhelming.
- Have an ongoing 'to-do' list up on your wall and tick off the tasks as you do them, regularly reviewing and adding new ones to keep up momentum and stay focussed.
- Have a weekly calendar up so you can plan ahead, prepare for the different activities and see what's due as well as review past achievements. Don't stress if you fall behind, just edit your calendar and to-do list accordingly; life happens and sometimes with all the best intentions things don't go as planned.
- It has been noted that to form a new habit, it takes 30 days, so start with one new positive behaviour and consciously repeat it daily until it becomes a habit. Choose something productive that will improve your life—it can be something

small such as saving money in a tin or a practical task like writing a page of a blog or journal.

- Make yourself accountable for achieving that one goal.
- The way we carry ourselves makes an impact—walk tall, smile, look people in the eyes and let your natural kindness shine through.
- Identify a person you admire and believe are successful in life and note how they conduct themselves. Ask them for advice—how do they stay motivated from day to day and succeed?
- Begin to look at yourself more kindly; have some compassion and become you own best friend. This will take time and perseverance. What may help are daily affirmations and listing all of your positive traits. That should boost your confidence enough to stay motivated.

Here are a few to get started with:

- I am worthy, I matter, I have a lot to offer, I don't sweat the small stuff, I appreciate the beauty in life, I am grateful for what I have, I am intelligent, I am valued and loved, I am respectable, I deserve love, I deserve success, I am awesome; I am kind, I am compassionate, I like… (Insert things you like about yourself) about myself.
- Remember that you don't speak to anybody as much as you speak to yourself in your own head, so be kind. What you tell yourself, you will come to believe. So feed it positivity, nurture it and offer it love and acceptance. At the end of the day, the only opinion that matters is your own; the minute

you begin to like and accept the whole of yourself, life becomes easier. You need to get out of your own way.

- Make time for self-care like taking a walk, having a duvet day, coffee and a chat with mates, booking a massage, etc., which will inevitably enhance your life and boost your self-esteem. We live in such a busy world that it's important to take time out for rest and relaxation.

- Do not fear failure—it promotes growth. If you don't make mistakes, how will you ever learn how to improve? Even a famous celebrity like Steven Spielberg was rejected three times from USC's School of Theatre Film and Television, but he never gave up—he kept trying and persevering until he became who he is now. A world-renowned film director. Consider how you can channel your failures into success. If you want it bad enough, never give up.

- Don't go it alone—if you need help, just ask; give others a chance to offer support. Sometimes it helps to have a mentor or nominated person who helps you stay on track. Pretty much like a personal trainer helps people in the gym with their exercise plans.

- We all know how tedious the more boring tasks can be, so in order to make them more bearable plan treats in between for achieving the more mundane tasks. Celebrate the small victories and accomplishments!

Negative Thoughts

Self-Blame: We often blame ourselves for what goes wrong in our lives, particularly in early childhood incidents, which in reality makes no sense. As a young child, how can you be held responsible for the break-up of your parents? Or the depression of your mother or father? Or the addiction of alcohol or drugs within the family home? Or a tragic accident that resulted in losing a loved one? Or that you were abused? These are just a few examples of what people have shared with me that they felt hugely responsible for as young children growing up.

The solution for this type of thinking is to place responsibility where it belongs—it was never yours to carry. You were the child. You had no control over the situation or choice in the matter. Stop carrying burdens that don't belong to you. If you ended up role-reversal parenting your parents as a child, you may have felt forced to grow up faster than your peers and shouldered adult burdens and traumas you were not ready for or able to carry.

Would you expect your own 6-year-old child, niece or nephew to carry shame, guilt or blame for any of your current adult mistakes? No. Exactly. So, as an adult looking back, recognise you were innocent and accept none of it was your fault. You cannot be held responsible for your parents' mistakes.

Feeling Unworthy: As a child, if you were made to feel insignificant or 'invisible' due to a hectic family lifestyle, parental conflict or emotionally unavailable parents, you may have felt feelings of inadequacy and unwittingly carried that into your adulthood as a core belief about yourself. I have had many a client share thoughts of feeling unloved, as if they were in the way or the cause of their family's problems.

The solution for this type of thinking is to remember that each one of us—no matter how outwardly destructive or how inwardly judgmental we are of ourselves—we inherently have goodness within us. Nobody is born bad, useless or unlovable. Instead of over-analysing or worrying about your perceived weaknesses or what's missing in your life, recognise the many blessings you have and all of your strengths. Everybody has positive attributes; it's a case of highlighting the good stuff! You have every right to be here, you do matter and you are worthy.

Trying Too Hard to Fit In (even when it means going against your own values)**:** Nowadays, there is a lot of focus on how to look, dress, talk, eat etc. We live in a fast-paced society that promotes material success. Social media plays a heavy role in influencing us at every level from what we see on TV to posts on Instagram, TikTok, Facebook, Twitter and the hundreds of other sites all vying for our attention and wanting us to conform to their version of style and reality. Trying to live up to societal norms in families, at school, and in the community can become an overwhelming feat in this day and age where everyone and everything is so accessible. It's enough to cause anybody to question who they are and what they stand for.

I have worked with many a teenager undergoing an identity crisis because they feel they are not enough; the peer pressure makes them feel that they 'should be' better than they are. They are unhappy with themselves because they think they need to have a better body, prettier face, more expensive wardrobe or own the latest tech. They struggle to accept who they are, constantly chasing an image of what they think they should be instead of accepting who they actually are and working to develop themselves. This rejecting of the self then results in a conflict between the head and the heart and has side effects such as anxiety, depression, low self-esteem and a sense of non-belonging.

Although I have used teenagers as an example for this, there are plenty of adults in the same position who question their own worth and value in comparison to others around them, making them feel inadequate.

The solution for this type of thinking is to break the rules and make your own. Be unique and start your own trend. Remember people only post snapshots of 'happy' moments on social media. Nobody really posts awful pictures or unhappy moments—therefore, it is a false sense of reality. It may seem like everything is okay in their world, but I can assure you, everyone has challenges and difficulties in life. As for celebrity photos, know that a lot of time, attention and make-up goes into airbrushing pictures to make them look immaculate. Again, fake—not real—images of how they actually look.

Poor Role Models: When you don't have strong, positive role models growing up you can develop unhealthy patterns of behaviours, particularly if one or both parents suffered with depression or anxiety themselves. Watching them as children, you may have picked up negative ways of coping with stress and learned them into adulthood as a coping mechanism yourself. This could include self-defeating behaviours, not accepting one-self, feeling inferior and supressing emotions.

The Solution: It's never too late to identify a positive role model of your own choosing. Pick somebody you know personally or someone famous whose values, personality and beliefs you really admire. Ideally, people who are confident and who love, accept and care for themselves openly and feel comfortable in their own skin. Then, just follow their lead. If you can, then reach out to them and ask for support. If you can't identify anyone, then create your own role model. Write down the personality traits you want to emulate and start incorporating them into your daily life.

Conditional Love: If you have made self-acceptance a conditional love, based on how much you can achieve before you allow yourself to be fully accepting of you, then this is a recipe for disaster. The fact that you feel you have to achieve X-amount of things before you deserve to be fully accepted by yourself is a self-sabotaging behaviour. For example, you won't consider yourself worthy of acceptance until you get a higher paid job or own a house and have expensive furniture. Or until you complete that degree you started. Or until you settle down, marry, have children, etc. When is it enough? How do you measure your success?

The Solution: Remove all the conditions that are holding you back, then accept all of you, and instead of 'waiting' for the conditions to occur celebrate each target as you achieve them. Develop healthier ways of measuring success and take into account life's little blessings and achievements, like smiling at others and being helpful, not just the big stuff like graduating or getting a job. Appreciate all the things you have achieved so far, big and small, and give yourself credit for all of that first. As for the other stuff, aim to achieve your desired goals step by step in manageable chunks and remember that some things are in the hands of fate, which is outside of your control.

There must be something wrong with me: I have dark thoughts / unacceptable traits / secrets. This issue is not unique to you. Believe me when I say this issue impacts every living soul. We all have a dark side and under the right circumstances, it may arise. Usually, though, it can be kept in check. We each have varying degrees of issues we struggle with daily, inwardly and outwardly. For some it is anger; for others it's an addiction or compulsive thoughts or behaviours. What you must understand is that this darker side of you exists for a reason; try exploring it, understanding it, accepting it's there and not punishing yourself for having it.

The Solution: Remember that everyone is waging their own wars—we all have our own demons and you are no different. As such, nobody is perfect; we are all a work in progress just trying to get through each day intact. Allow yourself to gradually learn self-compassion and understanding for this part of yourself. It's not the enemy, it just needs reassurance from you that things will be ok. So much healing can come when you embrace the shadow aspects of yourself instead of rejecting them. If it's too scary to try alone, seek professional support via therapy. They may just be outdated defence mechanisms that used to keep you safe but have now become an obstacle. Remember, your thoughts do not define you. Use humour if you have to; its ok to laugh at yourself and begin to embrace all parts of yourself, which will in turn unleash your personal power.

Personal Power

If I were to ask you here and now, "Do you feel you have power in your life?" How would you answer? What do you think of when the term 'power' is used? Is it a positive or negative feeling for you? What experiences of power have influenced your life? Do you see power as a destructive, abusive force, or a strong and positive force for good?

Our personal experiences of power will often dictate how we feel about it. For instance, a child growing up in an environment of domestic abuse may associate power as a negative term as the abuser was powerful over others. In contrast, a child who grew up in a family wherein choice was offered, and they were consulted during decision making for family affairs may feel power is a positive force. It nurtured their ability to feel valued, important and 'powerful' through having their voice heard by the adults around them. Power means different things to different people and can be interpreted in various ways. For the purposes of this book, I am exploring the concept of 'Personal Power'.

What is personal power? The definition can vary from person to person but the basic premise remains the same. Personal power involves strength and confidence in oneself and the ability to pursue what really matters to you. So, how do you know what really matters to you? Well, by filtering out other people's influences on your life you can reconnect with yourself in a way that enables deeper insight.

Have a think about what makes you truly happy; what makes your heart sing and keeps you motivated? This will help to focus you on your goals and promote your personal power to achieve what you want in life. Positive thinking, a good opinion of yourself and a willingness to learn and develop further encourages personal growth. This in turn increases feelings of self-worth and will empower you.

The more you recognise your own likes and dislikes and act on making things happen in your life, the more you will be able to deal effectively with adverse circumstances and start to see challenges as opportunities. We live in a highly competitive society that encourages ambition, and in order to keep up it's important to learn about our own strengths and areas for development so we can keep track of personal progress in every aspect of our lives. Knowing oneself is the key to success in life.

In order to really understand who we are and what we think, there is an activity that can help.

Exercise: For this activity, you need access to a clock and to have one other person with you, sitting in a quiet space facing one another. It can be a friend, family member or colleague. It's up to you who you feel comfortable to open up in front of. Once seated, you decide which of you will begin and act as the questioner. The questioner will then repeatedly ask the other person the same question, "Who are you?" for 10 minutes and the other has to answer by saying different things about themselves and who they are. After 10 minutes, you switch over and the person who was answering becomes the questioner for 10 minutes.

The rules are that you cannot repeat the same answer twice and once the labels of mum/sister/husband etc. are completed you need to reflect deeply on your core personality traits. It's amazing what you might say in this time—you have to dig deep for answers, and those I have performed this with have surprised themselves with what they share. The attention and focus being solely on you forces you to consider yourself in a way that's never been expected of you before.

Try it; you might just learn something new about yourself!

*"I am…humble enough to know I'm not better than anyone else, but wise enough to know I am different." (*Unknown*)*

Identifying Your Own Behaviours

Are you a people pleaser? Do you often put yourself to the bottom of the pile in order to help everyone else—often to your own detriment?

Does doing this then cause internal resentment towards those who do not reciprocate your kindness and efforts? If so, you may develop a further distance from your authentic self. So, instead of being silent and frustrated, your authentic self ('I') would make a point of telling others how you feel and that you would like more appreciation for your efforts and some reciprocation. Whereas in reality, your socially constructed 'Me' may not have the confidence to do so for fear of being rejected, disliked or losing others' approval. After all, you do what you do in order to fit in and belong, so why risk that by speaking your mind?

Why not, is what I would challenge. If you continue like this, you will never have your voice heard—and you'll continue to feel downtrodden in life. You have unwittingly put yourself in this position and only you can pull yourself out of it. Don't expect other people to change; change must come from within you. If you don't like something, it's up to you to act on it, not others. It begins with liking, respecting and accepting yourself.

You are worthy, you do count, and you are valued. If you believe in yourself, then nobody else can take that from you. It gives you a peaceful sense of calm and confidence that needs no words. All you need is to be more assertive; you can be very diplomatic in refusing and saying no. Try it—you will feel awkward at first, but you will get used to it. You have the right to agree or decline your time to help others; it's your life. Do not help others to your own detriment—if you are on the floor, you are no good to anyone, so keep a little energy for yourself.

Imagine a teapot when it's full. You can afford to pour some tea for others but as it empties out, only drips are left; you will need to refill the pot. In the same way, as humans, we need to draw back when our energy reserves are low and recuperate, rest, refill our teapots and then offer out support again. Just know when to stop and refill—develop healthy boundaries and a self-care routine that allows you to politely say no to others' requests of you when your pot is nearly empty.

So, have you fallen into any habits you do not like or feel pigeonholed into roles in life you did not choose or want anymore? If so, it's time for change. There are steps you need to take to achieve the changes required. Only you can decide what those changes look like and how you plan to achieve it. What I can provide through this book are tools to help you on your way; worksheets to help you change your life one step at a time, by addressing one issue at a time.

Let's begin by looking at generalised themes. In life, there are givers and takers; if you happen to be a giver and those around you are takers, you will soon begin to feel used and taken advantage of as people begin to expect the same level of commitment from you when giving little in return. If you are a taker, you may offer minimum support and expect maximum help from others to do things for you.

Takers are often life's charmers who get things done by appealing to the giver's natural inclination to help. The balance between both is a happy combination of giving and taking at regular intervals and not resorting to asking every time there is an occasion where help is needed. For example, an event is being planned locally—yet it's the same handful of people that put themselves forwards to help set up, tidy up, plan and organise it. They are the givers.

Takers will turn up, enjoy the event and disappear before the end to avoid helping out. Make sense? Recognise this pattern in yourself or others? This is a simple example, but it serves the purpose of highlighting the concept.

- So, do you act one way but feel another?
- How would you identify yourself—as one of life's givers or takers? (Try to evidence reasons why.)
- Are you happy to be that way? (Or, do you want to change, and why?)
- If you could change something about the way you are, what would it be?

Remember, all you need to do is say no, be assertive, and have respect for yourself and others by being open and honest. If you can help, you will, but only when you have the energy, time and ability. Love yourself the way you love others and show yourself that same willingness to help—only on this occasion you help yourself because if you don't look after yourself, nobody else will. Remember that self-care is not selfish; it is essential for survival.

Chapter 6

Regulating Your Emotions

Growing up, as children, we learn how to manage emotions from our parents/caregivers. After all, they are our first role models on how to manage life. If they had unhealthy emotional habits, this would be passed onto us inadvertently and some of it would become ingrained in us about how to act, behave, react and manage when facing difficulties. Every family has a dysfunction of some sort; it's what makes us unique. Some families have a 'brush it under the carpet' attitude to problems where children are taught not to dwell on core issues and act like everything is okay when it is not.

Issues are not acknowledged or dealt with—just hidden. These children are taught that expressing emotion of any kind excessively is bad or negative. They quickly learn to suppress their feelings and mimic the family system of not dealing with problems whilst growing ever anxious and uncertain of themselves.

In other family systems, children may have no boundaries and parents can for whatever reason (substance misuse/domestic abuse) be neglectful, so children grow up feeling unsafe and overly emotional— not able to regulate themselves in a healthy way. They can become excessive in expressing emotions and develop emotional, behavioural and social difficulties as a result. In these families, if caregivers are volatile emotionally then children learn to express themselves in a similar pattern. Each family system is different, as is each child, and whatever we pick up in our childhood can stay with us into adulthood as conditioned patterns of behaviours, thoughts and actions when relating to ourselves and others.

So, have a think now about your family system growing up as a child— how did they operate and how did it affect who you are? What stereotypes did you live up to? Were you the family joker? The agony aunt? The mischievous one? Or a Jack-the-lad type? Who labelled you, and do you still feel the constraints of that pigeonholed expectation from family members? For instance, 'Maya' had been the family mediator for years; anytime anybody needed help, or something done, they would go to her expecting her to help. She enjoyed the attention she got from this role and was happy to help growing up. But as she grew older, got married, had her own children and took on more and more responsibilities, it became a burdensome role.

Maya grew fed up of being the one to make everyone feel better and when she was in need, everyone was suddenly busy. Every time she tried to make excuses and justify that she was really too busy to run around after everyone her siblings wouldn't accept this and kept asking favours of her. They maintained that expectation of her to be the one that does everything for everyone. "Oh, leave it to Maya; she'll do it." That was her role. It seemed they wouldn't allow her to break the mould she was in, so after several attempts, she went quiet on them.

Maya stopped taking their calls and answering their messages. This made them angry and concerned, demanding to know why she had fallen off the radar. It was only after a while of this silence that Maya was able to be firm and tell her family how she felt. She told them that she needed time to herself and could only help a little, not like she used to because she was busy with her own family unit. Her family persisted a little after that but eventually got the message and asked her less and less. Maya still offered help where she could but no longer felt the pressure of having to be so accessible and available all the time.

It took Maya months of counselling and self-reflection to find the courage to break this cycle and come out of the mould she was placed in by others. Have a think now and consider Maya's story—have you repeated the cycle or flipped the script and created your own family system? Do you feel trapped in an old childhood family role that no longer serves you as an adult?

What happened as a result of Maya struggling to regulate her difficult emotions was a mixture of suppressing and over-indulging in feelings of anger, resentment, frustration, and sadness. On occasion, she had outbursts of volatile emotions one minute and silent brooding the next whilst that anger was bottled up. Neither of these worked. There was no balance until she sought help via therapy to find what worked for her.

One of my clients, 'Liz', was told as a child by her mother that 'angry little girls are bad girls and should never show their anger'. It is no wonder that as a child she suppressed anger and exploded as a teenager with a force of anger that led her to rebel against all authority.

As an adult, she has felt unable to express anger in a healthy way, going from one extreme of silence to emotional outbursts. Her core belief as fed to her by her mother was that anger is bad—so how can she reconcile that view with how she feels without critically viewing herself as 'bad'?

This viewpoint has led her to experience bouts of depression and anxiety throughout her life and managing anger is the main reason she entered into therapy. Once she recognised that no emotion is inherently good or bad, she was able to self-regulate and let go of what her mother had ingrained into her about the matter. She accepted that anger, just as any other emotion, is a necessary feeling that comes and goes for a reason.

Difficult emotions are often at the heart of almost every mental health issue. Have a think now about your own emotional regulation skills. How well do you understand and work with your emotions? Do you label them good or bad? Positive or negative?

What I have found working with people around matters of the heart is that many judge emotions as either inherently good or bad. This labelling further impacts the understanding and expression of that emotion. For example, many believe that joy, gratitude, hope, kindness and happiness are positive, whilst disgust, anger, sadness, shame and fear are bad.

What judging some emotions as bad encourages us to do is to avoid them rather than acknowledge and work with them. All emotions are essential for a healthy balanced life. To be fair, some emotions do feel better than others, but we need all emotions as tools to express ourselves. Each one has its place and to block any would create a conflict, compounding any existing mental health issue present within us.

All emotions are essential because they are indicators of how we feel; they impart a sense of being and provide us with emotional intelligence that we need to act on.

Tip: Watch Disney Pixar's Animation Movie "Inside Out" made in 2015—it depicts emotions in very relatable ways.

To illustrate how each emotion is necessary, consider this scenario:

A thief breaks into your home and tries to steal your belongings. If you had no anger how could you defend yourself and your family? If you had no fear, how could you regulate the adrenalin needed to act and force required to overcome the invasion? These so called 'negative' emotions are absolutely needed in such circumstances and in many others. So, before you prejudge how you are feeling, please acknowledge the why behind it—why are you feeling a certain emotion? What was the trigger and how can you process it to move forwards?

One of the reasons we think some emotions are bad is because we often confuse the emotion with the response or behaviour that follows it. For example, someone gets angry and becomes aggressive; we would be afraid of the violence displayed but, as a side effect, also blame the anger and become scared of anger, thus deciding that anger is 'bad'. We accept that aggression is often not a good thing, but aggression is only one of the many possible responses to anger; remember aggression (a responsive behaviour) is not the same thing as anger (an emotion or feeling).

We can, with appropriate support, patience and practice, learn new ways of responding to our emotions and create healthier patterns of behaviours and responses. Doing this will radically minimise hurt, pain and emotional turmoil, resulting in happier, healthier ways of living and relating to one another.

To truly embrace emotions, one must allow them, feel them, acknowledge them and let them flow and pass. Any emotions you need to release you will do so organically if you allow yourself the time to heal slowly without rushing the process.

There is a simple approach to managing emotions we can all master with the right attitude. Focus on recognising your current patterns—how do you normally react when somebody upsets you? Surprises you? Makes you angry? Shows you compassion? Pays you a compliment?

If you feel okay with your current reactions and don't wish to change, that's fine, but if you feel you could benefit from a different approach, then changing how you respond to emotions can be done; but it takes time. It involves increasing understanding of yourself, developing more self-awareness and new habits, then consistently practicing them over and over again until it sticks. Remember, they say it takes 30 days to form or break a habit. Try it.

To support you through this process, I have listed some pointers below:

1.   Try not to keep your feelings bottled up or suppress your emotions. They are there for a reason and need to be given acknowledgment. Prohibiting them can create inner conflict and compound existing mental health issues. You will find that by suppressing emotions, all you are doing is delaying a more major outburst further down the line when you least expect it. Anything can trigger it and you might find yourself emotionally overwhelmed during a routine supermarket trip. Our hearts and minds need to work in sync to promote a healthy balance in life.

2.   Allow the free flow of emotions as they arise and share how you feel with someone you trust or a therapist. Feelings are like visitors; they come and go and, like moments, they pass.

3.   Try to recognise, name and pay attention to the emotions you are feeling and when you feel them. They come up for a reason. Sometimes it helps to write about them, through poetry, song or via journaling. It can act as a reflective tool to track your thoughts and progress.

4.   Everyone has gut instincts and an inner voice. Try to tune into yourself emotionally and understand what the root causes are behind your emotions—why might you be feeling like this?

5.   Learn to recognise your defence mechanisms—if you use anger, self-pity, denial or procrastination as defences, are they working? If not, look at addressing the issues behind your emotions. Try to be proactive when considering your issues and start troubleshooting. Do what you can to minimise the issue and actively try to improve matters. After all, only you know how it feels to be you and will know what works and what doesn't for you.

6.   Understand through experience how each emotion makes you think and feel and what impact it has on you in that moment and any lasting effects afterwards. There are patterns and reasons for this—we live and are shaped by our experiences, so try to focus on what you need to move forwards.

7.   We all have the capacity for greatness and change, regardless of past adversities faced, or who you are now. Always do what is right for you. Sometimes, all you need is a helping hand. If you know someone who has your best interests at heart and loves you for who you are, then ask them for support to work through issues. This could be a friend, family member, spouse or work colleague. There are professional avenues for support via counselling and self-help groups. Check what is locally available in your area.

Having discussed at length how to regulate emotions, let's take a closer look at some actual emotions and explore what impact they have on you.

Sadness

Sadness is a strong emotion and, at its extreme, often results in depression. This includes a sense of hopelessness and extreme sadness; overwhelming feelings of despair, grief and low energy can be experienced depending on how sad a person is. As with any emotion, it is on a spectrum of mild to extreme. Some sadness visits temporarily for a specific reason and other sadness pervades the very existence of our being during times of distress and loss. It can cause us to feel empty. Sadness often arises out of a need that was never fulfilled, or a loss suffered or purpose taken away, such as losing a loved one, a marriage break up, a job loss, neglect by others, and many more scenarios.

Sadness can be so overwhelming it removes our energy to the point we have little or no motivation to tackle what's happening or change our lives. Sadness at its extreme can be hard to overcome.

Ultimately, sadness carries a message that reminds us we need to pause, reflect, allow the grief and then compose ourselves—as opposed to 'fixing' or doing things. Unfortunately, sometimes we lose ourselves in sadness instead of acknowledging it and learning from it. Sometimes, we overthink matters and feel hopelessly out of control and unable to find a way out of the darkness. What we must remember is that sadness is a necessary emotion and allows us to express freely our natural responses to trauma in life. It can sometimes be healthy to sit with grief and allow yourself time to think and be present, to actually feel the sadness so it is poured out of us and not stuck inside.

It's only when we lose ourselves to sadness and a darkness that we need to take action. Not because we have a mental health condition or label such as 'depression', but because there is so much more to life than trauma and loss. Just as there are trials and tribulations, there are blessings and beauty around us. Never lose sight of that fact; it's the universal law of balance. Think about the moon and stars that shine brightly through the dark nights and the beautiful flowers that bloom in spring. The meals out with friends and family filled with love, laughter and joy or enjoying hot chips on a cold night and cinema trips to watch your favourite movie. Soundtracks you dance to and enjoy relaxing to. Pets that love you unconditionally.

It's important to acknowledge all the simple joys in life alongside the troubles; it's what will keep you going and keep that flame of motivation burning slowly in the background.

To support you moving forwards, I have listed some pointers to help when it comes to managing sadness:

DO's

1.   Reflect on what you feel is missing in your life; have you lost anything?

2.   What will it take to make you feel fulfilled?

3.   Any hobbies or activities that make you feel alive?

4.   Make a bucket list of things you want to try in life and a vision board to help you stay focused on and motivated by your ambitions. Make a plan of how to achieve these dreams step by step so they can become a reality.

5.   Try and acknowledge your loss without losing sight of the bigger picture. Life goes on, try not to over analyse things or ruminate too much.

6.   Spend time each day socialising, even if it's a few minutes on the phone or going out to stay connected to other people and feel a sense of value, worth and purpose.

7.   Set yourself daily mini tasks to raise your energy levels—have a relaxing soak in the bath with your favourite book or walk down to the local grocery store and buy yourself a treat. Ask others for support when you need it.

8.   Keep humour alive; watch comedies or have chats with friends about funny memories.

9.   Do some research on topics that interest you online.

10.   Allow yourself to feel emotions and cry if and when you feel the need to. Don't block it. The body knows what it needs don't let your mind block the natural progress your soul needs to heal itself.

11.　　Seek professional help as and when needed, via your GP and health professionals if you need medication, and via therapists offering counselling to help you make sense of your world.

Try not to:

1.　　Overthink, overanalyse, or torture yourself, keeping yourself stuck in a painful moment over and over again.

2.　　Allow lethargy to spread and oversleep or become inactive for long periods of time.

3.　　Be alone for too long; the mind can play tricks on isolated people.

4.　　Use vices such as drugs or alcohol to cope—they will only act as band aids, temporarily numbing pain and then coming back even stronger as the root causes have not been worked on or processed.

5.　　Stay in this depressed state because it offers sympathy from others—this is classed as 'secondary gain' in psychological terms. Being extremely sad has a pay-off, which is others paying more attention. This doesn't last and eventually people tire of offering their time and sympathy. Try to be proactive and seek solutions and troubleshoot issues instead of being in a victim or martyr mode. Use support offered to rise up, not stay down.

Anger

What is your relationship with anger? Is it a familiar emotion, or one that you suppress? Can you control it, or does it control you? What is your worst fear around anger? Just a few questions to start you pondering on this emotion as it is one many of us struggle with. Anger gets a lot of bad press, but we need it in life, as illustrated previously, to survive. Anger can arise when we feel something is unfair; it can build in pressure so we feel it in our minds and bodies. Anger can trigger our defences, and we all react differently to anger. Some become aggressive and abusive, others will debate and argue their points, whilst some remain silent with a brooding anger and resentment that is suppressed.

Anger doesn't need to be feared; it is a part of us all and, when managed well, it can motivate us to change and develop as people. It incorporates a wisdom and opportunity for learning and growth unlike any other emotion. It teaches us so much about ourselves and others.

Next time you feel angry, try to track where it came from using these simple questions:

- Are you the type that holds their anger until you burst? Or do you get angry in a flash, but then calm down just as quick?
- What makes you angry?
- When angry, what do you do?
- What do you say?
- How do you behave?
- What techniques do you currently use to calm down?
- Why do I feel this way? Has something unjust occurred?
- Has it built up over lots of small things, or is it something I have felt for a long time?
- Is it something I want to take action about?
- Realistically, what can I do about it without harming myself or others in the process?
- Is it something that can be changed?
- Is it in my control or outside of it?
- If outside of my control, what can I do to manage and tolerate it?
- Can I learn to accept things the way they are?

Another thing to ponder on is how you react to anger. Are you the type of person who, when angry, lashes out to hurt others?

Or are you the type that hides in plain sight, suppressing it and avoiding the problem? 'Ostriching' is what I like to call it. When the head stays firmly in the sand, avoiding the issues and hoping that inaction will make the problem go away.

Are you able to address things head on and tackle problems as they arise?

Constructive anger can bring about positive change both on a micro and macro level. Just being assertive and discussing our issues with a respectful attitude, asking to be heard and behaving in a non-violent way can prove fruitful. In relationships, try talking about 'problem' issues when calm over a cup of tea, not when things are tense. Not when in the heat of anger. At this point, it's often too late to reason with one another. Try to learn about each other's boundaries. Tell each other when you are beginning to feel anger—send out warning signals and ask for support.

Try to breathe deeply and count to 5 or 10 before responding—give yourself time to calm down and think before saying something you may regret. Whatever you do, try not to resort to violence or disrespecting yourself or others; try not to judge and make others feel small. Don't bully or intimidate to get your point across, and don't ignore the problem; it will only grow and fester until you address it. Last but not least, try not to harm yourself or others; this includes self-harm, aggression and substance abuse. Problems can only ever be exacerbated by via drugs and alcohol. The temporary relief or numbing makes things worse long-term, adding addiction and financial / family loss to the overall picture.

As discussed earlier, we pick up cues in our childhood about how to manage emotions from those around us; this can help or hinder our progress into adulthood, depending on how they managed their anger. If being angry was a scary, volatile thing, we may shy away from expressing it. If anger was used to get things needed in life, we may use it to assert ourselves. If anger at home growing up was the cause for violence or substance misuse, we may follow through in similar patterns as parents are often role-modelled by children. It is about recognising that patterns can be changed and that you don't have to react in the same way. You can learn new ways of managing anger that are healthy and not abusive. Anger is a powerful emotion, but more powerful is the way you choose to manage it.

Some Tips

- **Always think before you speak**—Often, we do a lot of damage in the heat of the moment; what is said cannot be un-said or un-heard. Try not to say something you'll later regret.

- **Fresh air and physical exercise**—Going to the gym or taking a walk for some air can help reduce stress and help you to calm down. Whatever works; for some it may be putting on their favourite song and having a moment, while for others it could be punching a pillow, or even screaming into a pillow, or going for a jog around the block, thus removing themselves from the situation long enough to reset emotionally.

- **Explain your anger once you feel calmer and more in control**—In order to communicate your message so that others can hear it, do so once you are thinking clearly and can express your frustration in an assertive but non-threatening way. Share your concerns and needs clearly without hurting others or trying to control them.

- **Own your feelings**—Try not to use accusatory language that sounds like you are blaming or criticising (even if you feel like it). "You never help me, you just come and go as you please, using this place like a hotel!" Sound familiar? This may antagonise the situation. Flip the script and try saying, "I feel upset that the house is in a mess and would like some help with clearing up." It's about being respectful and specific and owning how we feel by using "I" statements. Also, try to avoid over exaggerating issues by using sweeping statements and over-generalising, like, "You never remember to put the washing out." It can have the opposite effect and cause more tension.

- **Explore possible solutions**—Try to think of how to make things better instead of getting worked up over what went wrong. Work on resolving the issue at hand. What caused the anger, and how can it be managed if that same scenario played out again? For example: Feeling overwhelmed with household chores? Ask for help. Draw up a schedule and delegate tasks to other family members so that the pressure is not upon you alone. Remember that anger won't solve any problems; it may make things worse.

- **Humour helps**—It is possible to use humour to diffuse tense situations. It can help to explore what's making us angry. Sometimes, we have unrealistic expectations for how we want things to be. In recognising this, we can address matters. Be careful that any jokes or humour used do not come across as minimising the issues, sarcastic or offensive. This could hurt people's feelings and make things worse.

- **Breathing and relaxation**—Try practising mindfulness techniques of deep breathing, meditating and visualising a calm scene. Maybe a favourite holiday destination sticks in the mind—lying in a hammock on a sunny, sandy beach beneath palm trees with the ocean lapping at the shore and fresh cocktails and exotic foods within your reach. (Works for me.) Music helps, so if you like, put on your favourite song. Some people enjoy being creative, so if poetry is your thing then read or write some poems, pen some lyrics for a song, or paint your heart out. You can also journal as a way of putting thoughts on paper. Do whatever works for you.

- **Improve communications by agreeing to disagree—** Sometimes we just cannot reach a resolution due to differences in opinion, but this doesn't mean that there is no way forward. Learn to respectfully agree to disagree and not force one's opinions on another. We are all unique and operate at different levels. Variety is the spice of life, so don't feel that your way is the only way forward; be open and receptive to trying new things. Most of all, respect that everybody is entitled to their own opinion.

- **Forgive and move on—**Try not to hold grudges. It takes up so much more energy to hate than to love. Forgiveness is freeing and can release you and the other person from the grip of negativity. If you can't forgive, that's okay too; just move on. Don't force yourself to feel something if it still hurts but try to at least move forwards and seek professional therapeutic support for cases like this. Unresolved trauma can keep us in dark places. Re-hashing over events can cause stuck-ness in relationships and result in an unhappy bitterness that feels horrible to live with. Be open and honest, share how you feel, and ask how the other person feels—in this way you can work together to find a resolution. Do so respectfully and you may both learn valuable lessons from the experience.

- **Recognise when to ask for support**—Controlling anger is a challenge for us all and every now and then, we could all do with some additional support, tips and techniques. It might be worth considering help with anger issues if, when angry, you become violent or aggressive, hurt others and/or feel out of control.

- Essentially, we all have a choice when it comes to anger and how we manage.

1. Stay angry and miserable, making ourselves and loved ones suffer.
2. Address the issues where possible in a constructive way.
3. When matters are outside of our control, we learn to accept the situation and let it go.

Acceptance doesn't mean giving up or approving of the problem; it offers you a release and emotional freedom. It takes far more energy to stay angry than any other emotion. It's like holding on to a hot coal that's burning through your soul. It can become toxic fast, and not worth making yourself ill over.

Shame

Shame is one of the most powerful hidden emotions. Its roots live in our past and its branches reach into our present and can extend into our future. Shame incorporates the morals and values that we learn as youngsters. The right and the wrong as highlighted through religion, society at large and different cultures we belong to.

It makes us focus on what we say, do, and think, and it helps to regulate how we behave. There is a level of good or healthy shame. For example, we wear clothes when we go out in public to cover our nakedness and protect our private parts. However, sometimes shame can be misused as a means to judge and control. Or we can develop our own distorted views on personal shame due to external influences or past abuse. This leads us to feel shame that is out of context and is toxic and emotionally harmful, causing us to harshly criticise ourselves.

At its worst, unhealthy shame can create a conflict within the heart and mind whereby victims of abuse take the view that they are somehow responsible for what happened to them. They may feel great guilt and shame that is not theirs to carry. In these scenarios, confusion over who is to blame ensues and victims can develop feelings of self-loathing. In this context:

Guilt = "I did a bad thing."

Shame = "I am bad."

Negative shame permeates our very souls, encompassing the whole of our belief system about who we are. This type of unhealthy shame can impact our mental health with long-lasting consequences beginning in childhood and stretching out into old age if left unresolved. It can cause us to harm ourselves and others physically, emotionally and psychologically. I have worked alongside individuals in therapy who have shared feeling like they are 'evil', 'damaged' or deserving of ill treatment because they think they must have provoked the abuser and are to blame. This distorted sense of reality lends itself to the development of several mental health ailments and can leave people feeling suicidal.

All adults carry feelings that are rooted in their childhood developmental experiences. Adult survivors of abuse may have particularly powerful feelings and memories from their abuse. These feelings can inadvertently be triggered by present-day circumstances that somehow remind them of the abuse, resulting in anxiety. Where the mind may block, the body remembers and felt emotions rise up, causing uncertainty of mind and emotional turmoil. Maybe as a child you never knew what to expect or how to act in social or family situations because of the abuse.

Fear and anger are both natural emotional responses to the threat of being assaulted. The after-effect is sadness and a sense of not feeling safe anymore as you recognise that your abuser (maybe parents or another trusted adult) could hurt and abuse you. This scenario gives rise to shame and guilt; such emotions tell you that you still hold yourself responsible for what happened. It is a heavy burden to carry as a child and grows with you into adulthood. Often rage appears as the built-up frustration of anger that could never be safely expressed within your family home growing up. Frustration is the feeling you are left with when nothing seems to go your way, and confusion is a sign that you don't know why it happened or what you can do about it.

The disappointment you may have felt towards others for their failure to protect you may have created a sense of apathy and emotional distance. As a child you may have felt a sense of helplessness, hopelessness and powerlessness, which caused you to stop trying to find safety and to accept life as it was—a crippling belief that it was never going to get any better. Survivors often use a number of defences to numb out the pain whilst some might adopt a "workaholic" lifestyle to avoid painful feelings. Others may try to "push down" the feelings by overeating or turning to alcohol or drugs to escape from reality.

For healthy recovery, it's essential to be able to regulate the intensity of these feelings—this can be achieved by monitoring your emotions daily. Try to develop the habit of asking yourself what you are feeling at different times of the day. Have a list of emotions and feelings you can use as a checklist and make a note of anything that you felt strongly about. Try and identify what situations might have caused you to feel this way and explore your reactions. They might be bodily felt emotions, internal thoughts, or even flashbacks. Journal about it; writing it out can feel cathartic. Or use a voice recorder to record your thoughts. This will help to clear your head and process your feelings better.

As survivors of abuse, remember to place responsibility where it belongs—with the abuser. All the negative emotions of shame and feeling responsible or to blame really belong to the perpetrator who hurt you. It's not your fault. They were wrong. Not you. It's okay to let go of the guilt and shame; it was never yours to carry in the first place. Start to trust yourself again and look after the parts of your wounded soul that have felt so alone for so long. We all carry within us our younger selves, our inner child. Know that you are safe and can take care of yourself—soothe your inner child with words and acts of love, compassion and reassurance and become your own champion. Team up with your inner child and support each other to face the world moving forwards.

Read inspirational quotes and stories of others who have had similar experiences to remind yourself you are not alone and to motivate you to create a positive change in your life. If you are struggling with this issue, seek support from people you trust and get professional help via therapy.

Anxiety

Anxiety can be described in many ways as it impacts people in different ways. However, what it has in common across the board is the element of fear. An unsafe feeling inside that causes physical and psychological symptoms. We feel afraid when we don't feel safe. In genuine cases of danger, fear and anxiety can help as they are necessary emotions to keep us safe. However, fear and anxiety can remain long after the danger is past—yet our defences remain in place, causing us to feel stuck in anxiety.

In order for us to manage effectively, we need to learn how to be safe again and recondition our defences to work for us and not against us. The flight, fight, freeze defence mechanisms are alive in us all and it's our brain that commands our bodies to react in a specific way when we feel threatened.

- Flight: Run away or hide; the instinct to get away from the danger
- Fight: Attack the threat; the instinct is to defend oneself through violence.
- Freeze: ('Disassociate'): When you go numb, don't move, and fear grips you to the spot. Some may mentally float away whilst the body remains rooted on the spot. This is dissociation and many who have been abused often dissociate to cope.

It does very much depend on the situation as to what reaction you may have when feeling threatened, based on what type of threat it is. For instance, feeling intimidated by a boss at work may elicit a feeling of wishing to disappear (go off sick) or to fight back. It all depends on your own personality and defence system. In a home invasion situation, you may freeze, particularly if being threatened with a weapon; or, your instincts may take over and you run, or stay and fight while defending your property. So many variables, and you won't know which you will do until it happens.

I believe that knowledge is power, and so understanding why you feel threatened in any situation can bring clarity on how to manage and what to do.

- Draw up a timeline from birth to your current age and list what factors may have caused you to feel such a strong fear or anxiety over the years.
- What are the triggers?
- Have there been times, maybe in your childhood, when it was not possible for you to make yourself safe?

- Have you been in unsafe situations over long periods of time in the past?
- If so, then the defence mechanisms that may have worked for you back then are no longer effective now and have become a hindrance to your healing process.
- It could be that your fear responses are due to an unresolved issue from your past that returns because it has not been addressed.
- It is important, therefore, to understand the historical reasons of your fear and to explore/address them in a therapeutic environment.
- Do not isolate yourself or punish yourself by ruminating over past wrongs; instead, actively seek to redress them.
- Do not turn to alcohol or drugs to cope as they will only make things worse, and the problems will still be there when you become sober and are no longer high.
- Always seek medical support if the issue is deep rooted and you need additional support via your GP.

Check what your unhelpful thought processes are and address them as they arise. In the next chapter, I have listed a few of these; see if you recognise any.

Chapter 7

Unhelpful Thought Processes

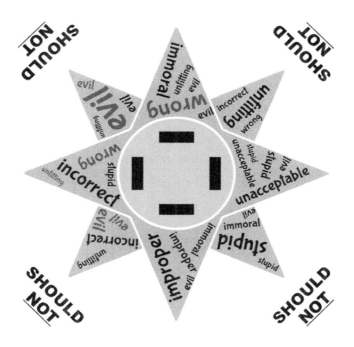

There are a number of common unhelpful thought patterns that can be quite irrational when people become stressed. Under pressure, we can distort reality and over worry, exaggerate and begin thinking in unrealistic ways about things. Our judgment is affected because we are so exhausted from worrying about the problem; then, habitual negative thought processes take over, causing us further anxiety.

Don't worry if you recognise yourself doing any of these—there is a way to remedy it, and I will offer techniques on this.

Black & White Thinking: This is when we think about things as definite, either one extreme or the other. Pretty or ugly, intelligent or stupid. As you can see, there can be many in-between descriptors to these statements, but it becomes inaccessible to a person locked into this type of thinking. It can be fraught with difficulty as it forces the thinker to pick a side; there are no happy mediums. This can distort reality, making a person believe there are only set options when there can be several if they opened their minds to it. Always and never feature a lot, and over generalisations can create a false sense of reality.

Solution: Try to change this habit by listening to what you are saying in your own mind. Pause for a moment and hear your thoughts—what negative messages are being played? Acknowledge that you are in the black and white thinking mode and make a conscious effort to reframe your negative thoughts into more realistic ones. For example:

"I recognise I'm doing that black and white thing again because I think my boss is evil. I blame her for not inviting me to the work to-do. Its more

true to say I'm hurt by the fact I wasn't invited; she can be quite inconsiderate but that doesn't make her evil, just thoughtless."

Now, you try and use the above information and write a scenario you have experienced of black and white thinking and how it can be addressed:

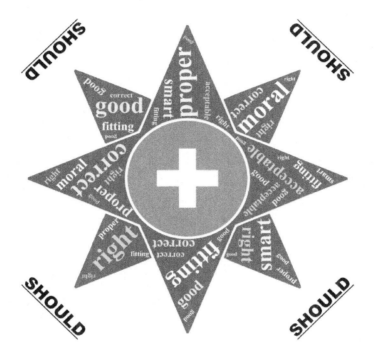

I MUST or SHOULD habit: "I must be the absolute best all the time in my job or studies, otherwise I am incompetent and useless."

"You should behave as I expect you to, otherwise you are disrespectful and deserve to be told off."

Sound familiar? If such thoughts occupy your mind, you may struggle with the concept of accepting things the way they are and not trying to control everything and everyone around you. Nobody can control another person's thoughts or behaviours, but they can control themselves.

Solution: Instead of thinking that when things don't go your way, it's all bad, try to reframe thoughts to accept a range of options. "I would love to be the best manager at work, but I accept I have limitations; however, I will still try regardless. That's all I can do and hope for the best."

"I accept that I am a work in progress and will address the bits of my life I am unhappy with to achieve the change I need to feel happier."

Thinking like this will replace the old, negative black-and-white thoughts with more fluid and colourful options to consider; you will become less harsh on yourself and others.

Now, write a real-life scenario you struggle with in your thinking and how it can be addressed:

Problem thought:

_____

_____

_____

_____

_____

_____

_____

Alternative thought options:

_____

_____

_____

_____

_____

_____

_____

_____

_____

_____

_____

_____

_____

_____

_____

_____

_____

_____

_____

Emotional Reasoning Habit: In this thought process, it is often assumed that how we feel is fact and not something we can change. That is incorrect. "I feel really low and this means I must have done something awful to feel so bad."

"I feel extremely angry and therefore I can justify lashing out at others, saying and doing whatever I want to."

Feelings come and go; they are fluid and not facts. Emotional impulses can lead us to believe things are factual in the moment but if you have a pre-existing habit of self-defeating thoughts and behaviours, then this process of thinking the worst can become debilitating.

We are all hard-wired with the ability to act when we feel threatened; the fight/flight/freeze concept we talked about earlier. These are our physiological reactions to stress and fear. Our body releases hormones like adrenaline and cortisol which pump through the body, making us feel physically and emotionally ready for any threat. Think of the cave men fighting sabre tooth tigers. This chemical reaction of fight and flight would help keep them alive. However, in today's society, we are not battling with sabre tooth tigers; it's more stress, fatigue and anxiety from daily living.

However, pumped full of these chemicals, we react in our fear and anxiety; the feelings can become overwhelming. We do not need such high doses of adrenaline that our bodies release and therefore remain in a state of anxiousness long after the perceived threat is gone. Symptoms of this are physical and psychological, such as rapid heartbeats, feeling nauseous, feeling faint, thoughts of impending disaster and feelings of being out of control and frightened. Panic or anxiety attacks can follow as the body tries to regulate itself in the aftermath, and breathing can become difficult.

The thing is, we can inadvertently go into any of the fight/flight/freeze modes during the day depending on the situation we are in and how stressed out we feel. It can create physical symptoms of feeling ill and psychological stress by overthinking matters.

Solution: The way to combat this thought process is to allow for other interpretations of what is happening—not going straight to the worst-case scenario but having an open mind and considering all the possible outcomes and options available. Recognise when you are going into that mode and learn your triggers and behaviours so that you can catch them before it's too late. Develop coping strategies by giving yourself time to think and be aware of what you are feeling; does it match the circumstances you find yourself in, or are you worrying unnecessarily?

Is it a life or death situation? Try to track how you are feeling and what you are thinking and if it is an appropriate way of managing. Does your reaction fit the scenario? Is it exaggerated? What is the reality of the situation? Put things into context. Explore what is really going on and accept that you will have a reaction emotionally and physically due to the hard wiring we all have.

Use a deep, slow breathing technique—in through the nose for 4-5 seconds and out through the mouth for 6-7 seconds. This gets more oxygen to the brain and helps the body to calm down. In order to calm the mind, tell yourself that you are safe, nothing can harm you, then repeat this internally or out loud if in private. Accept that your body is doing what it needs to in order to cope and release the stress hormones built up—just focus on breathing and allow the process to happen. Then, try to change your mood: take a walk, have a cup of coffee, call a friend, listen to a favourite song, repeat positive affirmations, take a shower and relax; do whatever it takes to change your circumstances in that moment and you will naturally calm down.

Creating a self-soothe kit for moments of anxiety can help. Contents can be transportable in a small pouch in your pocket so it's accessible wherever you. A photo of a loved one, a smooth pebble you can stroke, and essential oils you can sniff, like lavender to calm nerves. A fidget spinner or cube, your favourite gum, your favourite soundtrack loaded on to your phone. The idea is to use all of your senses to calm down.

Try the 5, 4, 3, 2, 1 Technique; it's a grounding exercise for managing anxiety. Name:

- 5 things you can see
- 4 things you can touch
- 3 things you can hear
- 2 things you can smell
- 1 thing you can taste

Now, pick a real-life scenario you have experienced and write about how it can be addressed differently next time using insights from above:

_____

_____

_____

_____

_____

_____

_____

I Know What People Think habit: "She thinks I'm stupid."

"My boyfriend thinks I am horrible."

"What a cow; I bet she did that to hurt me on purpose!"

Can you relate? The ramblings of our minds often cause us to make assumptions about others and pre-judgments that are not entirely correct. Believing that we know what others are thinking is a flawed notion and one that will inevitably get us in trouble.

Consider this: if everything in your life was going well and you were happy, would you have this habit of thinking the worst of others?

There is truth in the fact that we often project our own views and thoughts onto others and judge others by our own standards. This can be positive if you are a happy-go-lucky type of person but can be negative too for those who have low opinions of themselves and others. Suspicious thoughts and presumptions about others are often born out of our own insecurities and vulnerabilities. Nobody knows another's thoughts or intentions. Therefore, if this is your reasoning when deciding a matter, that may be flawed. These are your thoughts, not theirs—your own assumptions about what <u>you</u> think that they think. Not factual at all.

Always thinking of the worst-case scenario so that you don't have to take any chances in life can keep you stuck where you are not happy or achieving your potential.

For example: "I'm not going to even bother applying for that job even though I have the qualifications for it; nothing ever goes right for me, so what's the point. I'll just stay where I am and make do." By trying to save ourselves from disappointment we block our own path to success, change and growth. This form of defence is negative and keeps us down. This form of negative inner dialogue is unhelpful and cannot be trusted; it affects our mental health in a detrimental way. At the end of the day, nobody knows the future, and unless you change your own circumstances, matters will remain the same. Self-sabotage is harmful and such behaviours encourage ignorance and avoidance, which will keep us stuck in a negative cycle of despair.

Solution: Rather than viewing everything from a negative lens, try to open up and be flexible about your thoughts. Is there any evidence to back your thoughts? Explore if it is fact or opinion. Consider what other possibilities exist and allow them into your thoughts. What if you could flip your inner dialogue from, "life is rubbish", to, "life can be whatever I want it to be, all I have to do is try". And then, plan how you intend to improve things, take action, plan an intervention so that you take matters into your own hands and begin to live life according to what makes you happy and fulfilled.

There's no point in complaining about things if you do not address them or challenge your own negative thought patterns. Have a better opinion of yourself and this will rub off on others, and eventually those negative impulses will be replaced by more positive thoughts of confidence and self-belief, compassion and acceptance of who you are. Think positive; it has enormous benefits for the soul and sends out good vibes that are reciprocated in nature. If you give out good, generally speaking, you get good back and vice versa. Universal law of Karma.

Now, try and use the above information and write a scenario you have experienced of this thinking and how it can be addressed:

_____

_____

_____

_____

_____

_____

_____

_____

_____

_____

Drama & Over Exaggerating habit: "Oh, no, my hair looks awful!"

"I just got outsmarted by a colleague; they are so horrible"

The above statements reflect how we view our world, and the above self-talk is largely negative and over exaggerated. Having a bad hair day does not make it 'awful' and being outsmarted by a colleague does not make them 'horrible'. Why does our mind jump to such strong conclusions about things?

Does life have to be so dramatic? Can we resist making extreme statements and too much out of minor issues? If this is a habit of yours, consider how you talk to yourself; what is your inner voice saying? What messages do you say to yourself that create such drama? Why do you attach such significance to seemingly small matters? What events cause these behavioural responses?

If you tell yourself that you "can't cope" or feel "stuck and can't move on", then you are sending those messages to your brain, which in turn processes it as fact and keeps you stuck in a negative loop. You become the very thing you don't want to. It's like a self-fulfilling prophecy; you say it, believe it, and become it. For instance, if you say to yourself, "I will never be able to drive; I'm too stupid", then you will internalise this belief, which will prevent you from trying to change and keep you in that negative mind-set.

Solution: You can change this thought process by challenging it and developing a more positive habit of using less negative dialogue. "I can try to take my driving test and if I fail, I will try again until I pass." It's all in the language we use and the attitude we adopt towards life. Having a 'can do' attitude will take us a lot further than a 'can't do' one. Learn to use more appropriate language that is fair to you.

For instance, "I know when I blame everything on myself and feel awful it's just a habit I use to make myself feel justified in my sadness. It would be more appropriate to accept that I have had a lot to deal with recently but will get through it. It is what it is—not anybody's fault. I will be okay; I just need some time". This is a healthier inner dialogue that promotes self-acceptance and growth.

Now, write a scenario you have experienced of this thinking and how it can be addressed:

_____

_____

_____

_____

_____

_____

_____

_____

_____

_____

_____

As important as the dialogue we have within ourselves is, the dialogue that we have with others shapes the relationships we have in life. The next section focuses on how we are in relation to one another.

Chapter 8

Relationships

All healthy relationships require a balance of give and take. It's when we give too much of ourselves or too little that problems arise. We all have our own personal boundaries and knowing the bottom line helps when entering into any relationship. To what level are you comfortable compromising or sacrificing for the sake of the relationship, and is it at your own expense?

To help answer this, it's useful to know what the word relationship means—being in relation with another. The primary relationship everyone has is with themselves and then with parents, siblings and so on. Therefore, by the time we enter into romantic relationships we will have already formed several other types of relationships in which we have decided how to interact. This will in turn impact on our romantic relationships in many ways. For example, if a child grew up in a home where parental conflict was a daily thing, then their world view of adult relationships would be coloured by these experiences. They may repeat these behaviours and patterns in their future relationships as it was their version of 'normal'—their blueprint for normal family life.

In contrast, those who lived in happier homes with loving, stable family units could emulate that in their futures. Children learn what they live and only some break the cycle and don't automatically repeat. In order to maintain healthier relationships, it's important to know what things we should not give up when entering into relationships:

Your Identity: You are unique and as such will have your own way of being. This way of being has led to somebody else liking or loving you, so only change if you want to and for yourself, not for others, as that type of change never lasts. After all, you are the one that has to live in your skin and face yourself daily. If you feel okay just the way you are, then don't feel pressured to become something else. Own who you are with pride and allow yourself to be seen and heard for who and what you are.

Your Happiness: Being in a relationship is meant to make you happy, not unhappy. If you are currently in a relationship but are unhappy, then question why this is. Also question why you are still together. Having a happy relationship doesn't mean being happy all the time; it means being able to share your sadness, joy and experiences and feel safe and supported by the other. It also means being able to maintain your own identity within that relationship. Not being joint at the hip but being independent and dependent at different intervals.

A level of interdependence is necessary for closeness as it's the key to all relationships; people communicate to become closer to one another. Interdependence involves balancing your and your partner's needs within the relationship, recognizing that both are collaboratively working to be present and meeting each other's needs in caring, considerate and meaningful ways. If your relationship takes you away from things that make you happy, then it's time to take stock and evaluate if you are in the right relationship for you.

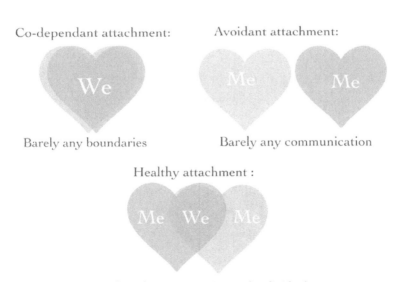

Co-dependant attachment:

We

Barely any boundaries

Avoidant attachment:

Me   Me

Barely any communication

Healthy attachment :

Me We Me

Shared communication and individual interests outside of the relationship

Quality Time: Remember the golden rule when dividing your time between your relationships with others. For those of you who are part of a couple, or married with children, consider the following factors:

Me Time

Family Time

Couple Time

Each one is as important as the other. If you are single, then this will still apply as Me Time, Family Time, Friends Time. Please see below for an explanation of these.

Me Time: It's important to spend time alone to reflect on matters big and small. Time to be with yourself and have no distractions. To think, meditate and feel present. We don't often get much alone time, especially in this day and age where technology makes everyone way too accessible. Every once in a while, try to schedule in some time alone. How you spend it is up to you. Just do something you enjoy. Relax while watching your favourite movie or read your favourite book. The idea is to re-calibrate with yourself.

Family Time: We are social beings and as much as alone time is healthy, it's equally important to spend quality time with family and friends. It's fulfilling emotionally, socially and psychologically to feel connected to those we love and care for. What better way of celebrating this fact than spending time enjoying each other's company? Do fun activities together or settle in for cosy nights in front of the telly.

Families can be a source of great joy and often great pain, but without them we would struggle to exist. We are all connected and as such take the good times along with the bad, working on difficult relationships as we go. Nobody is perfect and we will not all get on all of the time. We just accept each other for who and what we are and tolerate the differences where possible. The art of agreeing to disagree can prevent many an argument.

Couple Time: This one is particularly important for couples who have children and busy lives. If you spend all your time working and looking after the children, the relationship between you can erode over time, causing all sorts of difficulties. Some report feeling bored, distant, or unseen; monotonous routines can kill the joy in relationships that were once sparkly and fun. Life happens, and as the responsibilities pile up of bills, school runs, and work stress, it's easy to forget the needs of one another.

Please stop and take a minute to consider if you are in this situation. If so, then make a conscious effort to schedule in a date night or even a date day at least once a month if not fortnightly or weekly if possible. Go out away from the children and reconnect as a couple. Remember who you were before the kids came along; enjoy it being just the two of you again for a short while. Choose what you want to do—dinner, movies, spa, mini holiday away, or stay home but have kids taken out by family. Do whatever kind of 'date' makes you both happy. Alternate if you both prefer different things and take turns choosing the date activity.

The idea is to spend quality couple time to celebrate the love you have for one another. Don't wait for anniversaries or birthdays that only roll around once a year. Make it a regular thing. If money is tight, then do small things like a cosy meal in and drop the kids to a family member.

Your dreams and ambitions: Never compromise your dreams or ambitions. If you have a vision of achieving something, then stick to it. It is inspirational to see a person pursue their dreams and supporting each other in this is a beautiful thing. Working to achieve something you are passionate about gives you purpose; a focus and hope. To pursue your passion is to value your authentic self.

It takes a lot of energy, time, effort and planning to achieve such things in life. However, once achieved, the results are awesome; not only do you feel a sense of achievement and pride but by default, your partner can celebrate your successes with you and you, theirs. It's the whole package—the journey you go on to know what your passions are and then the time and actions taken. With love and support from others, it's a gentler path with a joint victory.

Your Voice: When we meet others, we often try to win their approval and sometimes this is by changing ourselves. If you feel you have to be somebody you are not in order to be with them, then you are not in the right relationship. Nobody should have to subdue their own voice; that is giving others power. Why should you become someone else or give up parts of yourselves in order to "hold on" to a partner? We are all worthy of love and deserve the best to and from one another.

What's the point in faking it? Any masks we wear will soon fall away and, ultimately, we can only be ourselves. If that is not good enough for your partner, then choose another who will love, care for and respect you for who and what you are. Never stay in a relationship where you can't speak your mind or feel free. If you feel controlled, undermined, unloved, disrespected or abused in a relationship, act now and address the issues, or leave the relationship.

Such toxic relationships will only affect your mental health in a negative way and cause low self-worth and low self-esteem and destroy any confidence you have. Remind yourself how much you deserve to be loved, by others and also by yourself. Relationships that are heathy provide us with greater security and confidence in who we are. They encourage feelings of safety whilst still exploring and discussing what each partner needs from the other.

Relationships are very much a two-way street, each providing the other with mutual love, respect and value. It's growing disconnected from who we are that causes us pain and inner conflict, resulting in poorer quality relationships with ourselves and others. How loved and accepted or unloved and rejected we feel as children by our parents or caregivers deeply affects how we develop our confidence, self-esteem and self-acceptance into adulthood.

Our past and childhood experiences shape how we seek love and whether we feel significant in the lives of others, or insignificant. Most of the emotional damage is done in the formative years. Absent parents, critical parents, abuse and neglect all counteract healthy development and attachment into adulthood.

How we attach to others is affected by how our parents offered us affection, time, and love from birth. Bowlby's attachment theory illustrates this well.

Chapter 9

John Bowlby's Attachment Theory (1958)

Knowledge is power, and once informed of something we can apply it to our own lives to make better sense of it. Therefore, I like to throw in some bits of theory to help foster a better understanding of matters. John Bowlby's Attachment Theory offers insight into how and why we attach to others the way we do. We can use this information and apply it in practice to see how we may have been affected into adulthood by our early attachment patterns.

In short, Bowlby believed that when a child is born, the primary relationship it has with its mother forms a lasting bond and the quality of that bond is dependent upon the mother's care and attention to the child, on her ability to meet the child's every need. If the mother is able to meet all of the child's needs and provides a loving, nurturing environment, the child will thrive and form a healthy or 'secure' attachment to the mother, which could be seen as a blueprint for that child's attachment pattern in future relationships.

However, in cases where the mother is unable to meet the child's needs for whatever reason and the maternal bond is weak or separated in early years, this can, according to Bowlby, cause long-term emotional damage. Bowlby classed this as 'Affectionless Psychopathy'. Bowlby described individuals suffering with this condition as having a lack of emotional development, illustrated by little concern for others, a lack of empathy, lack of guilt and an inability to form meaningful and lasting relationships.

Some argue that a stable network of adults, i.e. grandparents, uncles, aunts, and in single-parent families headed by fathers and not just the mother alone, can provide sufficient care for the child, counteracting negative outcomes. Therefore, this theory is not an exact science, more a possible predictor for emotional development.

Whichever family system you were raised in (single-parent, two-parent, extended family unit), it is useful to understand the lasting implications of how you were raised and what type of attachment developed as a result of your upbringing. According to Bowlby's theory, there are four basic characteristics that offer us insight into what attachment really is. They include the following, which are very evident in the relationship between a child and their caregiver.

1. Safe Haven

This is when the child can depend on their caregiver for reassurance, care and comfort at times when they feel afraid or threatened. For instance, new toys which startle the child due to loud noises or sudden movements when switched on could upset them. The child may cry, but the caregiver would hold and hug the child, removing the offending toy. This offers reassurance and making soothing sounds helps the child feel safe so they will stop crying.

2. Secure Base

In this stage, the caregiver would take their time and offer age-appropriate explanations of why the world is as it is. For instance, when the child questions the parent about why their sibling is unable to play outside due to illness, e.g. chicken pox. The child takes on board what the caregiver explains about the sibling being sick and unable to play. The child learns through experience and asking questions to make sense of the world around them.

3. Proximity Maintenance

This is about the closeness between the parent and child. As the child grows up and begins to explore the outside world, they maintain a closeness to the parent to ensure continued safety, comfort and reassurance. This can be a physical closeness, e.g. seeking parental hugs and affection, and emotional closeness, e.g. discussing school concerns with parents.

4. Separation Distress

This is about the pain a child feels when it is separated from the parent/caregiver. It can be emotional and psychological pain, resulting in the child crying or screaming when left at nursery by working parents. The child is unhappy about being separated.

Have a think about your own childhood for a moment. Can you relate to any of the above information and apply it to your own experiences of being parented?

The next bit will provide further information about the types of attachment styles we develop—how, why and the impact it has had on your life thus far. Read on...

Attachment Styles

1. Secure Attachment—Parental style: In tune with the child's emotions. Resulting adult personality: being able to form significant relationships; express empathy; and setting appropriate boundaries.

Children that are securely attached to their caregivers/parents tend to feel happier when around them; however, they become upset when they get separated from them. Even whilst in this state of distress, the child feels confident and secure enough in themselves to know that although his parent is away, they will eventually return. It is because this pattern has been repeated and the child has learnt to feel secure in this.

2. Ambivalent Attachment—Parental style: Inconsistent and sometimes intrusive parent communication. Resulting adult personality: feelings of anxiety and depression; feeling insecure and needing to control things; accusatory, irrational; and confused but also amenable and pleasant.

An ambivalently attached child can become extremely upset whenever separated from their parent/caregiver. The child feels unable to depend on their parent/caregiver when they need something. The child fosters a distinct lack of trust, safety and security in regards to the parent. As adults, we may be available one moment and rejecting the next.

3. Avoidant Attachment—Parental style: Emotionally unavailable, rejecting, cold and distant. Resulting adult personality: inability to express healthy emotions and avoids closeness/emotional connection; can be cold, indifferent, distant; critical; inflexible; impatient; and has low tolerance.

Basically, a child with an avoidant attachment will generally keep to themselves. They steer clear of parents/caregivers, and this may be due to possible neglect or abuse within the relationship. In order to keep themselves safe, they defend themselves using physical, emotional, psychological and social distance and becoming emotionally detached. As adults, they may become physically and emotionally distant in relationships.

4. Disorganized Attachment—Parental style: Parent is unable to function in the protective role as caregiver or meet the needs of the child. Parent may react to the child's fears by being frightened themselves or scaring the child further. Resulting Adult Personality: fearful, anxious, helpless, insecure and constantly seeking reassurance; also may be hostile and punitive when mirroring parental behaviours into adulthood.

This occurs when mixed messages are sent from the parent to the child due to confusing and conflicting parental behaviours and reactions to the child. It's a sort of mixed attachment style between the child and their caregiver. One minute, the parent is attentive and caring; the next, they are cold and dismissive. This creates a disjointed kind of confused attachment wherein the child remains uncertain and apprehensive, often developing anxiety in later life. As adults, we may not love easily and may be insensitive to the needs of our partner.

So, now that you have a clearer understanding of this theory and the differing types of attachment, you can apply this to your own life.

- Do you recognise any of the parenting styles described above?
- Can you see the results of it in your life now?
- Are you now a parent yourself?
- Have you repeated or broken the cycle?
- What is your attachment style with your own children?

The point in me adding this section to the book is to offer insights and lessons about attachment and how they can help us to heal as adults. We are not stuck in a mould and can very much re-write our life scripts, creating our own choices in life. What we must remember at all times is that personal development and learning is an ongoing thing; we can only improve our lives by trying, learning, remaining open and accessing the information and support we need how and when we need it. That can be achieved via self-help books like this one, professional counselling sessions where needed, and through supportive friends and family networks.

We all have gut instincts, and this provides us with the feeling of knowing inherently what is right or wrong for us. It's those years of experience so far that have shaped who we are and kept us going. We can use this to continually improve our relationships moving forwards.

It is when we are able to recognise the negative patterns of behaviours, triggers and thought processes that have resulted from our insecure attachment bonds that we can start to address our issues and end their effects on our lives. Just by acknowledging them, we make space for change and a healthier attitude towards future relationships with more in-tune attachments.

How to heal:

1.   Start by getting to know yourself. Write a list of personality traits you like about yourself; this will help re-build self-esteem. Find new ways of spending quality time alone to reflect on your life and, in equal measure, enjoy time around loved ones. Work on becoming your own best friend and give yourself a break from personal criticism. Be kind to yourself and tune down the negative internal voices; try to replace with a kinder voice of compassion. Take care of yourself and start doing things that make you happy. Make a list of things you have always wanted to do and begin doing them. Create a vision board and start to think about what you want to achieve in life.

2.   Work out what you are passionate about and keep doing the things that you enjoy. Art, photography, travel, studying, languages. Whatever makes your heart sing.

3.   Remember to look after every aspect of yourself; this includes your physical health as well as your emotional and mental health. Eat well, exercise and take up a hobby you enjoy—bike riding /

swimming/forest walks/gym sessions or even taking the dog for a walk offers fresh air and exercise.

4.   Practice mindfulness and meditation. It can help to ground you when life becomes busy and chaotic. Pause and allow the here and now to sink in. What is good about your life right now? What blessings exist in your life to be thankful for? Practicing gratitude and patience can create a sense of peace within the mind and heart.

5.   Allow your mind to wander and reflect on insights learnt from lessons in the past and present. Nobody can change your life except you. If something is bothering you, then address it. If you need support, ask for help from friends or family. If that's not possible, seek professional support via therapy.

The next section looks at how we operate within our own consciences and what they reveal about our true natures.

Chapter 10

Consciousness

What comes to mind when you hear the word Consciousness? Does it conjure up images of the brain, or a mystical spiritual energy? It can mean different things to different people, so for the purposes of this article, I will offer the dictionary definition:

"Consciousness is the state of being aware of and responsive to one's surroundings."

This means that we use our sensory perception to know and recognise things. Our sight, smell, and touch all work together when we are consciously aware. In effect, we all have two parts to ourselves: the conscious and the unconscious self. So, if being conscious means being aware, the opposite would be true when describing the word 'unconscious', or not being aware.

To highlight this point, let's explore a learning theory. Basically, when we study or learn new skills, we go through the following 4 stages of learning:

1. Unconscious incompetence

2. Conscious incompetence

3. Conscious competence

4. Unconscious competence

An example we can use to illustrate the above in simple terms could be as follows:

A learner driver has unconscious incompetence when taking their first lesson as they do not know how to drive, having never driven before.

After a few lessons, they move to the conscious incompetence stage— they realise or are conscious of how little they know as they continue to learn and practice driving.

Nearer to the time of their driving test, after many lessons, they become consciously competent as they have learned the skill of driving but are not fully aware of their ability, hoping that they are skilled enough to pass their driving test.

Let's say this person then goes on to pass their driving test and has been driving for a few months—they move into the unconscious competence level. This is where they become so competent that they no longer have to think about what they are doing when driving; it becomes second nature. The term 'autopilot' comes to mind.

Have you ever gotten into your car to go somewhere and arrived quickly, without realising how you got there? That's the brain performing at an unconsciously competent level, allowing your conscious brain to attend to more pressing thoughts and leaving the body and unconscious mind to do the driving.

People can become conscious of unconscious things. For instance, in Post-Traumatic Stress Disorder (PTSD), the brain has a habit of pattern matching—it puts together sensory evidence of the original trauma. Therefore, if during the original trauma of being mugged a car had been driving past at the time while beeping its horn, or a cat had been mewing in the background, then in the event of these things occurring again at a later date, a person suffering with PTSD could find that each time those sensory things are present in that order together, they act as a trigger and can cause them to become traumatised again. This is because the brain pattern matched the original trauma to the current day's event due to the similarities in sensory evidence between both events, creating anxiety and triggering the flight/fight/freeze mechanism.

This, in turn, heightens the anxiety and can cause a physical reaction as well as having a psychological and emotional impact. Constantly living in the fight or flight mode is exhausting for anybody, and it is in understanding how this works and why we are stuck in these patterns that will eventually free us to change our patterns of behaviour and think/act differently in the moment.

The past does not have to define our future, but in some cases it can and does. It is our conscious mind that collects good and bad habits as we repeat them over time, conditioning our brains to act, think and behave in certain ways. These things can be changed with conscious effort, time and awareness.

Being mindful is one way of challenging our negative processes. Mindfulness is attentive practice and it can help if we engage in at least 10 minutes of daily mindfulness practice, which is to sit and reflect on the day and be here and now, in the present.

Being mindful is about teaching your subconscious how to function. Try practicing being present and mindful for just 30 seconds. Focus on what you are doing in this present moment—notice with all of your senses of sight, smell, hearing and touch the moment you are in right now. Really focus on the present and notice your breathing. What do you see, smell, and hear? How do you feel?

The truth is that you cannot be constantly mindful or present. That is difficult, but you can have flashes and moments of it. Be mindful of your present task and think of thoughts as a dandelion—once blown, they scatter in the wind, blowing around silently in the background. To be mindful, you could choose one of those flying pieces (thoughts) to focus on and be mindful about.

So, moving forwards, how do you get motivated in a moment?

Well, there are five specific questions that you can apply to any scenario in order to plan ahead:

1. What would you like to have happen in your life?

2. What would need to happen for those things to be achieved?

3. Is there anything else that needs to happen?

4. Can you do what needs to happen?

5. Will you do what needs to happen?

Activities like this can help you get un-stuck and move ahead in life.

Self-Acceptance

There has been much talk in this book about self-acceptance; this is essentially you evolving into a way of being that fits your authentic self. How do you achieve it? Well, the concept is about accepting yourself, warts and all; the good, the bad, and the bits you hide. The key is acceptance without judgment. If you are your own worst enemy, then you won't get far in life. You imprison your potential and unleash harsh criticism upon yourself, making you feel smaller and lower in confidence and self-esteem. Basically, you self-sabotage.

So, consider now, do you put yourself down or find fault with yourself before anybody else can say anything? Are you afraid of being caught out and disliked for aspects of yourself you keep hidden? Do you like how you look, your personality, your values, and spirit? If you met yourself, would you be your friend? It's so easy to fall into the trap of self-depreciation and often, it is used as a defence. The thought being, "Well, if I say it first then nobody else can hurt me". The point is they probably wouldn't have said it anyway, so all that you end up doing is saying horrible things about yourself to others. Often, it's done so automatically you don't even realise you are doing it unless or until somebody points it out.

I had a client, 'Miranda', who was constantly doing this, from the moment she sat down for her session to the end; finding ways to berate herself and justify her own negative thoughts about herself. They were entrenched into her belief system from a young age. She was told by her mother that she would never amount to anything and was 'clumsy' and 'thick'. She was then bullied at school, which compounded her belief, and into adulthood she suffered with a nervous disposition and anxiety.

She felt she was not worthy of existing and would always put herself last on the list; her family would often put pressure on her, expecting her to do the lion's share of tasks. She soon realised how unhappy she was with everybody's expectations of her and feeling taken advantage of instead of valued that she ended up in therapy and suffering with panic attacks. She felt unable to regulate her emotions because she had lived a lifetime of suppressing them.

Through therapy, she began to find her voice again; she began a journey of change and recognised that how she thought of herself no longer needed to be dictated by others. She was able to see how the labels she lived with were not her own—they were placed on her and she believed in that as the truth, making it a self-fulfilling prophecy.

Meanwhile, her self-esteem was on the floor and she was afraid to say how she truly felt for fear of disapproval or rejection by loved ones. She realised that how she perceived herself was unhealthy. She was able to change her inner dialogue from critical to kind and remove the negative lifelong labels given to her, instead replacing them with positive attributes.

Having read the above case study, I want you to consider and become aware of what's occurring in your mind. What are you saying to yourself?

- Do I have a healthy way of relating to myself?
- Does how I think of myself make me feel like I can manage life's challenges, or do I feel overwhelmed and out of control and feel like I will forever be stuck in anxiety?
- Is this what I want?

"Surrender, one could say, is the inner transition from resistance to acceptance, from "no" to "yes." When you surrender, your sense of self shifts from being identified with a reaction or mental judgment to being the space around the reaction or judgment. It is a shift from identification with form – the thoughts or the emotion – to being and recognizing yourself as that which has no form – spacious awareness." – (Eckhart Tolle*)*

Relaxation Techniques for Stressful Times

- Deep colour combined with 'Square' or 'Tactical' Breathing.

Inhale through your nose for 4 seconds. Fill your diaphragm and notice your stomach rise as you inhale fully whilst visualising a pure, powerful energy. Hold for 4 seconds, then exhale out your mouth for 4 seconds, then hold for 4 seconds, visualising a toxic red breath of stress and worry—see it leave your body and release all that negative energy. Feel yourself calm down. Do this for a few minutes until you feel better.

- Tap positive affirmations using your fingers against your hands.

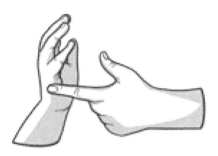

Using two fingers of one hand, tap on the side of the other hand gently and rhythmically whilst repeating positive affirmations. "I can do this, I will succeed; I am calm; I will be ok; I am focussed; I have a plan; my worries will not overpower me; I am strong; I am able; I will get through this", etc. Use your own words and be as creative as you like—but only use positive affirmations for this.

Safe Space:

- Visualise in your mind your favourite place. This can be a holiday destination, a made-up place, or your own bedroom. Picture somewhere you feel safe, happy and free. Use all your senses to picture the scene in your mind's eye; recall what can you see, smell, hear, taste or touch in this place. Whilst visualising this place in your mind, gently press your thumb and index finger together and rub together as if you are rubbing butter through flour repeatedly to anchor the memory for approximately 5 minutes.

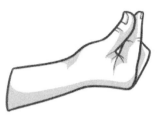

This way, you can escape to your safe place at any time of the day or night in your mind. All you need to do is to rub your finger and thumb again and you will instantly be taken back to your favourite place in your mind and have those calming feelings that come with it. It helps if you need to calm down. Try it—this technique can be used anywhere at any time. It's also quite discreet.

- Give yourself a Butterfly Hug.

Cross your arms diagonally over your heart and touch each of your shoulders and rub your arms up and down, slowly and gently, in a soothing motion as if you are hugging yourself; it's very comforting and calming. Whilst doing this, you can say to yourself reassuring words of kindness and compassion like, "I am ok, things will work out". This personal hug is great for times when you need to reconnect with yourself—it warms the heart and soul.

Gratitude

As we are nearing the end of our journey of self-exploration together, I would like you to consider the concept of gratitude.

Gratitude Journal:

I want you to take a few minutes daily, maybe in the evenings, to write down five good things about your day in your journal.

They don't have to be big things or grand gestures, just everyday things that you feel blessed to have, be or experience. It could be as simple as seeing an old friend again after a long absence or enjoying a favourite movie with a loved one. Or, even facing a challenge and overcoming it using your increased self-awareness and skills.

Write a Thankyou Text, Letter, or Email:

Reflect on your life so far. Who has inspired you, supported you, and helped you when you really needed it?

Who has had a major impact on your life? Consider someone who you would like to thank, or someone who you appreciate having in your life. With them in mind, put pen to paper or type out a text to show them how much you appreciate having them in your life and how much they have helped you.

Include specific details about what it is you appreciate about them and why you feel blessed and grateful to know them. If you wish to do this in letter form, then consider visiting them and hand delivering it to them; nothing beats face to face communication. If you prefer, you can read this letter to them when they are with you or if they live far, you can call them and read it out loud for them and then send it to them to keep as a memento.

For those you live with, notice the small daily acts of kindness you are shown by them and show your appreciation by thanking them directly. Often, we take others for granted, especially those nearest and dearest. It might be a partner, a sibling or a colleague who always checks in with you and goes over and above to help you. It could be a friend who always makes time for you. Make a list of people you need to thank and do it with warmth and love.

Take a walk in nature and be grateful for nature itself.

Take a mindful walk in nature; notice the birds, the greenery or even the city streets and take in the sights, sounds and smells of the world outside. As you breathe in the air, feel grateful for the little things in life. Make a special effort to appreciate your surroundings. You might notice the smell of freshly ground coffee or freshly baked bread from local bakeries. You might notice the birdsong and how the breeze of the wind is soothing on your skin. Spend a few moments taking in the sights and smells—use all your senses to appreciate nature's beauty all around you.

If you follow any particular faith, say a little prayer in gratefulness to God or the universe around you. Send out positive vibes whatever your belief system is.

Conclusion

"It's hard to practice compassion when we're struggling with our authenticity or when our own worthiness is off-balance." (Brene Brown)

Having read through the contents of this book, I now invite you to slow down and allow yourself to process your thoughts and feelings. I want you to start focussing on hearing your own inner voice and addressing your troubles. To have a better understanding of who you are and identify your most authentic self. Recognise your inner conflicts and don't allow self-sabotage the opportunity to destroy your heart and mind.

Recognise the toxic inner voices and expel them, for they do not belong to you—they were most likely planted by others. Then, replace them with the kinder, more compassionate voices of those who love and care for you and your own positive thoughts. Learn to become your own best friend. Practice the art of believing in yourself, have self-compassion and forgive yourself for past mistakes; let them go so you can heal. Trust your own judgments and create your own positive inner dialogue wherein you speak kindly to yourself, not harshly.

"What brought us depth and character are the very things we are often ashamed to talk about, namely, our inferiorities – being bullied on the playground, some physical inadequacy, an abuse inflicted upon us that we were powerless to stop, our failure to achieve what we'd like to in life,

an addiction we can't master, and many other small and big wounds and bruises that helped shape our souls." (Ron Rolheiser)

If you can offer yourself that validation internally, then nobody outside of you can take this away. You will no longer need to search for others to approve of you—the biggest approval is self-approval.

Or, as Whitney Houston put it in her song, "The Greatest Love":

"Everybody's searching for a hero, People need someone to look up to

I never found anyone who fulfilled my needs, A lonely place to be

And so I learned to depend on me, I decided long ago

Never to walk in anyone's shadows, If I fail, if I succeed

At least I'll live as I believe, No matter what they take from me

They can't take away my dignity, Because the greatest

Love of all is happening to me, I found the greatest

Love of all inside of me, The greatest love of all

Is easy to achieve, Learning to love yourself

It is the greatest love of all"

Become your own hero.

To all those of you who are reading this book, know that you are uniquely you; there is nobody else out there like you. Embrace that specialness and accept all parts of yourself; create your own destiny and be sincere in life. Don't distract yourself by comparing yourself to other people—it only takes away precious time from you to heal and develop yourself.

"By accepting our imperfections, we begin to live a life of authenticity and truth." (Brene Brown)

Often, we seek in others what we appreciate and want for ourselves and are drawn towards like-minded people. As such, often the very things we admire in others are already present within ourselves. Just remember that nobody has all the answers; we are all human and, therefore, make mistakes.

We are all struggling with something or other and nobody knows your struggles as they have not walked in your shoes, so be kind to yourself and be kind to others. If you need any help, use your friends and family for support and, where necessary, see a trained professional and get the therapy you need. There are a variety of different types of therapy out there and further down I have listed a few mainstream ones for your information.

Before that, I have added a few of my favourite, most poignant therapeutic quotes for you to reflect on.

Quotes

Be the love you never received. Be the acknowledgement you never got. Be the listener you always needed. Look at the younger versions of yourself within you and give yourself what it is you always needed.

That is the first step to healing. If you want others to see you, You must see yourself.

-Vienna Pharoan

Be the things you loved the most
About the people who are gone.

Author Unknown

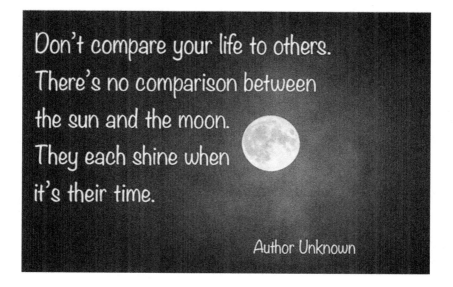

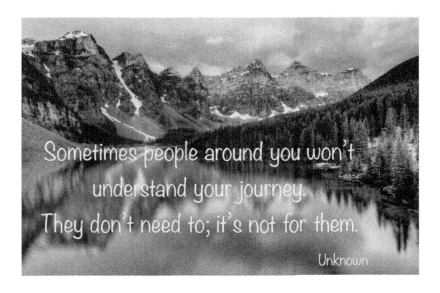

Whenever you find yourself doubting how far you can go, just remember how far you've come.

Remember everything you've faced, all the battles you have won, and all the fears you have overcome.

Author Unknown

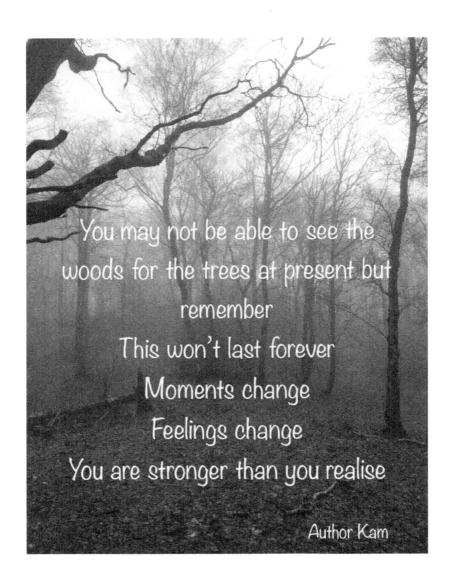

You may not be able to see the
woods for the trees at present but
remember
This won't last forever
Moments change
Feelings change
You are stronger than you realise

Author Kam

We are but a collection of people living in relation to each other

Author - Kam

The most sacred place dwells within our heart, where dreams are born and secrets sleep, a mystical refuge of darkness and light, fear and conquest, adventure and discovery, challenge and transformation. Our heart speaks for our soul every moment while we are alive. Listen... as the whispering beat repeats: be...gin, be...gin, be...gin. It's really that simple. Just begin... again.

Royce Addington

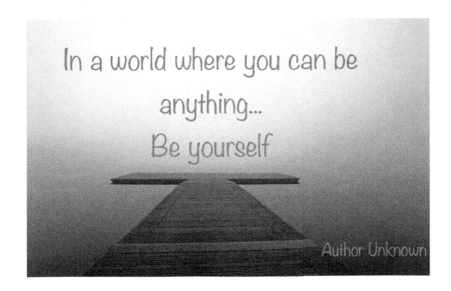

Types of Therapy

Person-Centred Therapy

This approach uses a non-authoritative style which allows clients to take more of a lead in sessions so that they will discover their own solutions. The therapist is non-judgmental and offers empathy and unconditional positive regard, acting as a compassionate facilitator—listening and acknowledging the client's experience without leading or taking the focus away from the client. The therapist is fully present to encourage and support the client by guiding them through the therapeutic process without interfering with the client's process of self-discovery. Open-ended questions help explore topics.

This promotes self-confidence, a strong sense of identity, trust and belief in oneself, and the ability to build healthy relationships with themselves and others. To trust his or her own decisions. This approach, alone or in combination with other types of therapy, can be helpful for those who suffer from grief, depression, deep-rooted trauma, anxiety, stress, abuse, marital difficulties and other mental health conditions.

The person-centred process facilitates your journey of self-discovery, and self-acceptance and provides a pathway towards healing and growth.

"Therapy is the arena of unresolved issues and unfinished business." *(Author unknown)*

Cognitive Behavioural Therapy

Cognitive Behavioural Therapy (CBT) is a short-term therapy directed at current issues and based on the idea that the way a person thinks and feels affects the way he or she behaves. The emphasis is on problem solving, and the goal is to change the client's thought processes and patterns in order to change their reaction and responses to tough situations. A CBT approach can be applied to a variety of mental health issues and conditions and is appropriate for children, adolescents, and adults and for individuals, families, and couples.

CBT can be used in combination or alone to treat depression, generalized anxiety disorder, post-traumatic stress disorder, addictions, OCD, anger issues, panic disorders, phobias, eating disorders, pain symptoms and many more.

CBT in practice incorporates learning to identify painful and upsetting thoughts about current issues and to see if such thoughts are realistic or irrational. If these thoughts appear to be unrealistic, the therapist will support you in learning new ways to process information and skills that can help change thought processes.

Homework is a big part of CBT and helps both the therapist and client track progress. The aim of CBT is to encourage clients to become more proactive in their own treatment so they can understand what is best for them to improve their lives.

"Time present and time past are both present in time future and time future contained in time past." (T.S Elliot)

Hypnotherapy & Mindfulness

Hypnotherapy is basically hypnosis under the guidance of a trained professional. It induces a calm state of focus and concentration achieved through relaxation, visualisation and talking techniques.

This relaxed state is likened to being totally focussed in a book, or captivated by a movie, music, or even your own thoughts. Whilst in deep rest, clients can focus their attention inwardly to identify and use natural resources deep within their subconscious that may help them to change or feel empowered again after a loss of identity. Hypnotherapy is often used alongside other forms of therapeutic intervention and it can be used to treat substance misuse, weight loss, addictions, anxiety, depression, phobias, sexual issues and unwanted behaviours and to motivate change.

It can also help with insomnia, communication, and relationship issues. It can support people with chronic pain to feel better and act as a calming influence for those under stress. The therapist will help you get into a relaxed, focussed state, ask questions about how you are feeling to support reflection, and offer positive ways that can help change the way you think and behave. Unlike media portrayals of pocket watches and pendulums, hypnosis is a gentle but effective way of addressing thought processes and releasing negative views. You will not be unconscious, out of control or asleep; you will hear the therapist's suggestions and it is your choice if you wish to act on them or not.

"Sometimes the heart sees what is invisible to the eyes." (Jackson Brown Jr.)

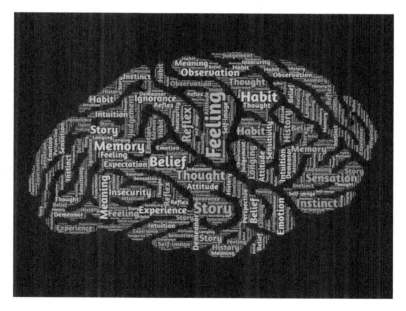

Neuro Linguistic Programming (NLP)

NLP therapy involves all of the senses and the use of appropriate language and articulation that supports behavioural change. It improves the client's self-awareness, confidence, communication skills, and social interactions. The aim of NLP is to help the client focus on their world view and see how it impacts themselves and others. It promotes self-reflection and insight to help change one's thoughts and behaviour patterns that cause negativity and block progress. NLP is useful when treating addictions, fears and phobias, anxiety, low self-esteem, PTSD and identity issues.

NLP therapists may use different techniques such as visualization, scoring one's thoughts and feelings to track progress and forming mental images of desired outcomes using all of the five senses. The therapist may encourage the use of positive language over negative words and help you to recognise your inner critic. NLP therapy can be short or long-term, depending on the issues presenting and how the individual progresses.

"You can be whoever you want to be; the only person standing in your way... is you." (Kam)

<u>Sandplay Therapy & Story Telling</u>

These two approaches go hand in hand and are particularly good when working with children or adolescents, and even many adults who have suffered child abuse in their history have benefitted from them. Sandplay therapy is an intervention that involves the use of sand, sometimes water, and miniature toys that represent figures in the lives of the client. They use these to draw their stories in the sand, creating scenes of miniature worlds that reflect a person's inner thoughts, struggles, and concerns. Much of this is non-verbal; guided by the therapist, the client chooses their toys and sets the scene, explaining only if they wish to (story telling) what is going on in their personal story. It's useful for those who have suffered some form of trauma, neglect, or abuse.

"The soul is ever searching for the light of truth." (Kam)

Emotional Focussed Therapy

Emotionally Focused Therapy (EFT) is a short-term therapy that looks at adult relationships and attachment/bonding. Together, the client and the therapist explore patterns of relating to others and seek to create pathways to make more secure bonds and develop their trust to move relationships to a healthier, place. This approach is beneficial for everyone; children, families, couples and individuals in distress. It helps address negative emotions such as anger, fear, loss of trust, or sense of betrayal in their relationship. EFT can also help reduce symptoms of anxiety, depression or trauma.

The therapist will encourage you to explore your current emotional issues and then help you discover emotions that you may not realize you have. Sometimes, past resentments resurface, and vulnerabilities may arise that were blocked by the more immediate emotions in your current relationship. You will learn to express emotions in a way that will help you connect, rather than disconnect, with your partner or family member. This can change negative thoughts and communication styles to positive ones—sometimes this is done via tapping on meridian points to alleviate stress, guided by the therapist.

"Even in life's darkest hours we continue to learn, grow and reach towards the light." (Carl Rogers)

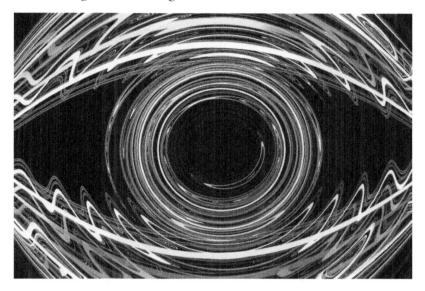

EMDR- Eye Movement De-Sensitization & Reprocessing Therapy

EMDR is a non-conventional type of psychotherapy created to eliminate bad feelings associated with flashbacks and negative memories from traumatic events. Unlike other types of therapy, EMDR deals with the crisis of emotions as opposed to the traumatic incident itself.

Treatment includes watching the therapist's fingers or a light bar that moves in different directions to stimulate the brain's responses and works on unblocking the brain when clients are stuck in anxiety, trauma or depression. It can also be done using headphones and listening to specific beats in either ear at regular intervals or via pulsating paddles held in each hand controlled by the therapist to stimulate the nervous system.

EMDR has been highly successful in treating severe trauma victims and frontline crisis workers such as soldiers, police, firefighters and medics. EMDR was originally developed to treat symptoms of PTSD, anxiety, and phobias. It can also be used to treat depression, eating disorders, addictions and sexual dysfunction. In this type of therapy, it is not necessary for the therapist to know everything; they work with the resulting negative emotions from your trauma, so you won't necessarily have to reveal all the details of your traumatic experience.

Through EMDR, negative emotions are addressed, minimised and often eliminated. Therapists will share techniques to help you deal with disturbing feelings and then guide you through a process known as desensitization. EMDR is effective quite quickly, and often only a few sessions are required to shift trauma until you get to a point where you can bring up memories of the traumatic event without experiencing the negativity that brought you to therapy in the first place.

The aim of EMDR is to fully process old negative experiences and filter out the emotions attached to those experiences. Thoughts and feelings that are no longer helpful or healthy are replaced with positive thoughts and feelings that will encourage healthier behaviour and social interactions.

EMDR therapy occurs in stages and is facilitated by the therapist in a systematic way, guiding the client through each phase addressing each negative emotion until those memories lose their power over them emotionally.

Buddha once said:

"What you think you become… what you feel you attract… what you imagine you create." Reflect on this and change your life for the better.

About the Author

Kamarun Kalam (aka Kam) is the creator of Talkwell Counselling Service. She was born and raised in Uxbridge, Middlesex and moved to Birmingham at age 11. Kam developed a passion for supporting others through her school's mentoring system and has been in the caring professions ever since. Kam has helped countless couples, children, families and individuals in her career as a social worker, Family Mediator and Psychotherapist spanning over the past 20 years.

In her downtime, Kam enjoys spending time with her family and taking spa breaks away with loved ones. She has a zest for life, a good sense of humour and loves learning new skills and techniques in order to help her clients in the best way possible. She is open minded and loves experiencing other cultures, cuisines, traditions and ways of life.

Her experience over the past 20 years has helped her to understand the human dilemmas we all face and the different ways we all manage our lives. Kam has helped many people to re-attune their lives and find their way through various struggles. Her warm personality, empathetic nature and quirky sense of humour puts others at ease. She is an outgoing, motivated and enthusiastic person who has a wealth of experience working with people from all walks of life.

Kam has worked with a number of professional organisations including the Salvation Army Contact Centre for separated families; as a Court Advisor for Children and Families Support Service (CAFCASS); Birmingham City Council as a Safeguarding Social

Worker; Barnardo's, supporting sexually exploited children; MIND, the mental health charity, as a Counsellor; and with the Youth Justice Service across the West Midlands. Kam is also a trained supervisor for Social Workers and Counsellors in training and has supervised several professionals across the span of her career so far.

Kam previously volunteered at her local radio station, Unity FM, producing and presenting a radio show on social issues to support local families by offering free advice and support, and has been a guest speaker on the Unity FM 'Approachable Parenting' radio show.

Kam currently works part time for FosterTalk as a Fosterline advisor supporting existing and prospective foster carers; she voluntarily contributed towards writing some of the content of the Mercy Mission 'Guide for Foster Carers Caring for Muslim Children'. Kam works the rest of the week as a Psychotherapist in her private practice, Talkwell Counselling Service.

Note from the author: *"I hope you have enjoyed my humble efforts to support you on your journey of self-discovery. Talk well to one another, take care of each other, and look after your hearts and minds."*

To learn more about me visit www.talkwellcounselling.co.uk.

If you have any questions about this book, feel free to email me at kam@talkwellcounselling.co.uk

I am also on Pinterest online:

https://pin.it/7fvwnx4pes547e

Instagram: @kamarunkalam

Etsy shop for Kensho Arts Digital Illustrations:

https://www.etsy.com/shop/KenshoArts?ref=simple-shop-header-name&listing_id=833587007

Wishing all of you a happy and fruitful life.

Printed in Great Britain
by Amazon